Grades 3–5

SHELL EDUCATION

Standards-Based
Investigations
Science Labs

Authors

Katrina Housel, Mary Beary, Josh Roby, Melinda Oldham, Judith Sise, Suzanne Ferguson, Cheryl Jakab, John Pearce, Peter Hope, Sue Barford, Faye Glew, and Ormiston Walker

SHELL EDUCATION

Credits

Associate Editor
Josh Roby

Assistant Editor
Leslie Huber, M.A.

Editorial Director
Dona Herweck Rice

Editor-in-Chief
Sharon Coan, M.S.Ed.

Editorial Manager
Gisela Lee, M.A.

Creative Director
Lee Aucoin

Cover Design
Lee Aucoin

Illustration Manager
Timothy J. Bradley

**Interior Layout Design/
Print Production**
Robin Erickson

Publisher
Corinne Burton, M.A.Ed.

Shell Education

5301 Oceanus Drive

Huntington Beach, CA 92649

http://www.shelleducation.com

ISBN 978-1-4258-0164-9

© 2008 Shell Education
Reprinted 2012

Table of Contents

Table of Contents *(cont.)*

Introduction and Research Base

Why a Focus on Science?

Over three decades ago, the American Association for the Advancement of Science began a three-phase project to develop and promote science literacy: Project 2061. The project was established with the understanding that more is not effective (1989, p. 4).

Inquiry-Based Learning

As Project 2061 began, researchers questioned the appropriateness and effectiveness of science textbooks and methods of instruction. Since textbook instruction puts more emphasis on learning correct answers and less on exploration, collaboration, and inquiry, the Association asserts that this manner of instruction actually "impedes progress toward scientific literacy" (1989, p. 14).

This same concern resurfaced over a decade later by Daniels and Zemelman (2004) who call textbooks "unfriendly." When most adults are choosing literature, they do not pick up their son's or daughter's science textbook. Daniels and Zemelman assert that today's textbooks are best used as reference books when students need large amounts of information on a particular topic within a subject area. Instead, they recommend the use of "authentic" sources.

Project 2061 recommends pedagogical practices where the learning of science is as much about the process as the result or outcome (1989, p. 147). Following the nature of scientific inquiry, students ask questions and are actively engaged in the learning process. They collect data and are encouraged to work within teams of their peers to investigate the unknown. This method of process learning refocuses the students' learning from knowledge and comprehension to application and analysis. Students may also formulate opinions (synthesis and evaluation) and determine whether their processes were effective or needed revision (evaluation).

The National Science Education Standards view inquiry as "central to science learning" (p. 2 of Overview). In this way, students may develop their understanding of science concepts by combining knowledge with reasoning and thinking skills. Kreuger and Sutton (2001) also report an increase in students' comprehension of text when knowledge learning is coupled with hands-on science activities (p. 52).

Values, Attitudes, and Skills

Scientists work under a distinctive set of values. Therefore, according to the American Association for the Advancement of Science, science education should do the same (1989, p. 133). Students whose learning includes data, a testable hypothesis, and predictability in science will share in the values of the scientists they study. Additionally, "science education is in a particularly strong position to foster three [human] attitudes and values: curiosity, openness to new ideas, and skepticism" (1989, p. 134). Science Labs addresses each of these recommendations by engaging students in thought-provoking, open-ended discussions and projects.

Within the recommendations of skills needed for scientific literacy, the American Association for the Advancement of Science suggests attention to computation, manipulation and observation, communication, and critical response. These skills are best learned through the process of learning, rather than in the knowledge itself (1989, p. 135).

Water Cycle

This chapter provides activities that address McREL Science Standard 1.

Student understands atmospheric processes and the water cycle

Knows that water exists in the air in different forms (e.g., in clouds and fog as tiny droplets; in rain, snow, and hail) and changes from one form to another through various processes (e.g., freezing, condensation, precipitation, evaporation)	*How Does the Puddle Change?* (Page 12) *Where Does the Water Go?* (page 14) *Where Does the Water Come From?* (page 16)
Knows that the Sun provides the light and heat necessary to maintain the temperature of the Earth	*Can I Build a Mini-World?* (page 17)
Knows that air is a substance that surrounds us, takes up space, and moves around us as wind	*What Is Wind?* (page 19) *How Can I Measure the Wind?* (page 21) *How Can I Measure the Wind Better?* (page 22)

How to Teach the Water Cycle

Dihydrogen Oxide

Dihydrogen Oxide, AKA H_2O, AKA water, is a familiar material which offers a wealth of opportunities for play and exploration. Students will have seen water in several different forms—liquid water, solid ice, and gaseous steam. Water changes state easily, back and forth, from one form to another. Other materials do the same—wax and chocolate, for example. But only water easily offers all three states—solid, liquid, and gas—in our everyday experience. And it's never possible to get the wax and chocolate back just the way they were!

Water

Water is the liquid state of the material. Liquid water is essential for life. Liquid water takes the shape of the container in which you put it, whether it be a bucket, cup, or jug. It flows downhill, but it won't go up except in a flood (although you can make a continuous column of water flow over and down if you use a siphon). Students will have had a lot of experience with water and its qualities in the bath, swimming pool, and ice cube tray.

Ice

Ice is the solid form of water. It is formed when pure water drops in temperature below 0°C (32°F). An amazing quality of water is that it expands as it freezes—tops are pushed off milk bottles and car radiators can be cracked. Frozen water takes up more space than it did as a liquid. As a result, the ice is less dense than water—the same amount of mass in a larger volume.

Steam

Strictly speaking, the billowing clouds that come from a boiling kettle are water vapor. Steam itself—water in its gaseous state—is invisible. You can see where it is by looking carefully at the spout of a boiling kettle—you can just see a clear space between the spout and the vapor. This invisible gas is true steam.

The stuff that fills the bathroom, making condensation run down the cold mirror and windows, is water vapor—liquid water in tiny droplets. It condenses on cold surfaces. This process is called condensation, and the liquid that condenses is called condensed water. However, if you tell your neighbors that you are having trouble with condensed water on your double-glazing, they may think you're a bit of a show off.

Lighter than Water

Water particles bonded together make ice. Unfortunately for the *Titanic*, ice is lighter than water. This is a very unusual but important fact that comes up time and again in this book. It is very unusual for a solid material to weigh less than its liquid. Apart from water, only a material called bismuth behaves like this. (You might have come across this pinkish metal if you have had a gastric ulcer. It is used in soothing medicines.)

Once you understand particle theory, you can understand why this should be. When water freezes, its particles form a kind of cage—a rigid pattern in which the particles are held away from each other. So there is more space in an ice cube than there is in water.

Where Does Rain Come From?

Rainwater isn't new. It's been round and round the water cycle forever. All of Earth's water is trapped in this endless cycle of change. When you drink a glass

of water, you can be fairly sure that at least one of the molecules at one time was part of the water drunk by a hero of yours, or by a historical character.

It's statistically likely. It has been estimated that a molecule of water from a glass poured into the sea at New York will wash up on the beach in California in a matter of months. On the way, it will have had amazing adventures—as part of the sea, a pond, a river, a cup of tea, or a glass of cola.

You don't have to look far to see examples of the water cycle all around you. Consider, for example, getting caught out in the rain. When you get home, you take off your wet clothes and put them in the washing machine. By the time you have done this, the weather has brightened up, and you hang the clothes outside to dry. The water returns to the sky. These simple actions demonstrate a simple water cycle. While the basic story of the water cycle is the same, the variations are enormous.

Water Evaporates

Molecules of water close to the surface are in constant movement. If they have enough energy, they break free of the water and lift into the sky. This can happen at any time. If you leave a saucer of water on a windowsill, meaning to put a potted plant in it later, the water will evaporate at room temperature. By the time you put the potted plant there a day or two later, the water level will have dropped. The water is evaporating.

Evaporation happens much faster if you put a bit of energy into the system. If you heat the water, the molecules get excited and break off with far more regularity. The water may "steam." It loses water molecules fast and if you are not careful, it will boil dry. The more energy you apply, the faster the evaporation. Boiling

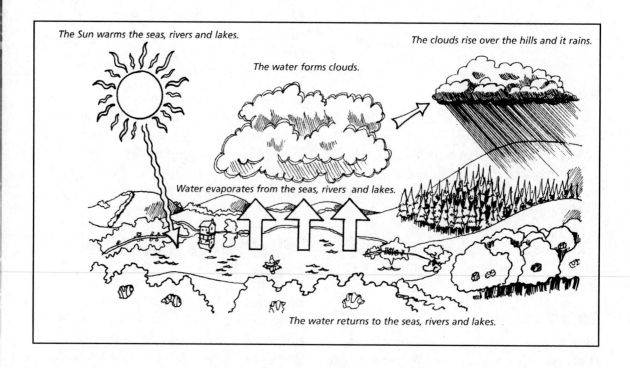

The Sun warms the seas, rivers and lakes.

The clouds rise over the hills and it rains.

The water forms clouds.

Water evaporates from the seas, rivers and lakes.

The water returns to the seas, rivers and lakes.

water is losing molecules fast. While they are above boiling point, the water molecules are actually a gas—water gas.

What's in a Cloud?

You have probably flown through a cloud if you have flown in an airplane. But you have also walked through one if you have seen mist or fog on the ground. Both clouds and mist are made up of water vapor, condensed into minute water particles that float in the atmosphere or roll across the hills.

As the water vapor rises, it cools, and it clumps or condenses, often around tiny dust particles. The smog of the big cities is caused by water condensing around waste from fires or car exhaust.

The cloudiness of water vapor is what makes it hard to see on misty days. If there is a fair amount of water vapor in the air, it is hard to see great distances. When you visit a hot, dry country, you may be astonished by the clarity of distant things and the sharpness of the colors. There is little water vapor in the air to spoil your view.

So the water cycle starts when the water around us—in the seas, rivers, streams, ponds, swimming pools, and even in that dish on the windowsill—evaporates from the surface and rises into the sky, to form clouds.

There's a big role for trees here, as they pull water from the ground and lose it through their leaves—a process known as transpiration.

A handy spin-off of this evaporation process is that the water that rises into the atmosphere is clean. It has left all its impurities behind. There are even rings of impurity left on that saucer. The pure water has gone up to form clouds.

Down Came the Rain

Clouds are unstable. As they rise and cool, the water condenses. Droplets run together to form bigger and bigger drops. Finally, these drops are so big that they can no longer hang in the air, and they fall as rain.

Condensing is the process of combining the water molecules. You see it taking place in your bathroom. Reaching a cold surface, water vapor from your shower condenses into water droplets, and these run down the mirror or window. We call these droplets (incorrectly) condensation. In fact, it is condensed water. It's the process that is condensation.

Up in the clouds, the condensed water droplets start to fall. Because this usually happens at quite a height, it is more likely to occur in mountainous or hilly places, or close to them.

If clouds are carried by the wind over high ground, they may rise higher and higher, getting colder and colder. The water vapor freezes. (Snow is frozen vapor, not frozen liquid.) and a crystal of ice is formed in these high clouds. As updrafts push the clouds higher still, more water vapor joins the crystals, and when they are too heavy to be suspended any longer, they fall as snow. If more water gathers around the frozen particle, it forms a hailstone.

Rivers and Streams

Once it has fallen as rain, the water's journey is far from over. Many possibilities arise. A droplet of rain may join a stream or river. It may soak into the ground, only to pop up somewhere else in a spring or well. It may scarcely touch the earth, hardly arriving before it evaporates away again.

How to Teach the Water Cycle *(cont.)*

Or it may start a long adventure that includes pushing a turbine around to generate electricity, being boiled for a cup of tea, passing through one or more humans, being cleaned in a sewage treatment plant, falling through a shower head, and being mixed with lemonade mix. It may wash your car, water your garden, or boil your potatoes. It may be drawn into a plant and combined with oxygen to produce more plant material and food for animals. Eventually, it may find itself back in the sea. And the whole cycle begins again.

A drop of water may travel thousands of kilometers between the time it evaporates and the time it falls to earth again as rain or snow. On the way, it may be partly responsible for some extreme weather conditions.

Storms

Thunderstorms are heavy storms with rain, thunder, and lightning. We usually get them in the summer because then the ground gets hot, and the rising warm air forms tall clouds with a flat "anvil" top. Electricity crackles in these clouds, caused by water particles rubbing together. When the charge has built up, it snaps to the ground as a flash of lightning. The air heated by the lightning flash creates shock waves that we hear as thunder.

Lightning travels at 140,000 km per second. That's half the speed of light. While the streak is very narrow (less than two cm wide), it can be 43 km long. You can survive being hit by lightning as long as it goes to Earth without passing through your heart. Park ranger Roy Sullivan claimed to have been hit by lightning seven times between 1942 and 1977.

Counting the seconds between flash and bang can give you an idea of the distance between you and a storm. Allow three seconds for a kilometer and five seconds for a mile.

Thunderclouds can grow to be 15–20 km high. Their anvil shape is caused by high winds at that height, blowing the top sideways. Some of the water in them stays unfrozen, even at minus 40°C. But clouds also contain fragments of ice that are growing onion-like, layer by layer. They then may become too heavy to be held up by currents of air and so fall to the ground as hail. If the air currents are really fast (as much as 145 kph), the hailstones may grow to the size of oranges before they drop from the cloud.

Hurricanes and Tornadoes

A hurricane (called a typhoon in the Northern Pacific and a cyclone in the Indian Ocean) originates close to the equator when a central calm eye is surrounded by inwardly spiraling winds. As the sea temperature rises, water evaporates into whirling, unstable storm clouds. A hurricane is a wind of force 12 or more on the Beaufort scale and is accompanied by lightning and torrential rain. Hurricane Gilbert in the Caribbean in 1988 gusted up to 320 kph. A cyclone in the Bay of Bengal in November 1970 caused the sea to rise ten meters, crashing into the Ganges delta to drown at least 300,000 people and one million farm animals.

The Seasons

Earth is going around the Sun. The time it takes to complete a full orbit—365 and a quarter days—we call a year.

Earth's axis is at a slight angle to the Sun. This angle stays the same as Earth orbits the Sun. Any point on Earth's surface will spend some of the year leaning towards the Sun and in strong sunlight. This is summer

How to Teach the Water Cycle *(cont.)*

in this part of Earth. It will spend some of the year leaning away from the Sun, and then it will be winter in this part of Earth.

Daylight hours are longer in the summer and shorter in the winter. Between the summer and the winter is spring, when daylight hours get longer and it gets warmer, and autumn, when daylight hours get shorter and it gets colder. On one day in the spring and one in autumn, day and night are exactly the same length. These days are called the equinoxes.

Daylight Times

In the summer, the Sun shines early in the morning. The evenings are long and children play outside until quite late. You may even go to bed while it is still light outside. Then in the winter, daylight time is shorter. The mornings are dark and you spend the evenings indoors.

Earth is tilted as it orbits the Sun. In the summer, the Sun appears in the sky for longer and climbs higher. In the winter, the Sun appears in the sky for a shorter time and does not climb so high. The changes in daylight time follow a pattern, and it is possible to predict this pattern to the minute.

Here are some sunrise and sunset times for London in the month of June 2000. The sunrise times are the time to the minute that the Sun rose. So on June 8, 2000, the Sun rose at 4:44 in the morning—nearly a quarter to five. The sunset times are the times the Sun set. So on June 8, 2000, the Sun set at 20:14 (8:14 at night), or nearly a quarter past eight.

Date	Sunrise	Sunset
1st	04:48 A.M.	8:08 P.M.
8th	04:44 A.M.	8:14 P.M.
15th	04:42 A.M.	8:19 P.M.
22nd	04:43 A.M.	8:21 P.M.
29th	04:47 A.M.	8:20 P.M.

How Does the Puddle Change?

Name _____

What You Need:
- jug of water
- chalk
- measuring tape
- warm sunny day

What To Do:

1. Watch your teacher pour water onto the concrete, then draw a chalk line around the edge of the puddle.

2. Note the time: _____

3. Draw the puddle and measure its perimeter.

Time: _____   Perimeter: _____

How Does the Puddle Change? *(cont.)*

What To Do: *(cont.)*

4. Draw the puddle when it has changed significantly. Note the time and measure the perimeter.

Time: _____   **Perimeter:** _____

5. Repeat step #4 when the puddle has almost disappeared.

Time: _____   **Perimeter:** _____

? Next Question

What might change the amount of time that the puddle took to disappear?

Notebook Reflection

Describe what happened to the water. Where did it go?

Where Does the Water Go?

Name _____

What You Need:
- electric frying pan with a clear lid
- jug of water

What To Do:

1. Pour water into the frying pan until it is about 3 cm (1 in.) deep.

2. Turn on the frying pan. Do not touch the hot edges!

3. Watch the water in the frying pan. Draw in the boxes what you see.

Where Does the Water Go? *(cont.)*

What To Do: *(cont.)*

4. Refill the frying pan and turn it on. Put the lid on top. Draw in the boxes what you see.

5. Turn off the frying pan and let it cool. Is there more, less, or the same amount of water in the pan?

 **Next Question**

Brainstorm what other things can be done and undone. What do they have in common?

 Notebook Reflection

Where did the water go the first time? What happened the second time?

Where Does the Water Come From?

Name _____

What You Need:
- ice cubes
- small container with lid

What To Do:

1. Put as many ice cubes as you can into the container. Seal the container.

2. Describe the outside of the container.

    _____

    _____

3. Leave the container alone for half an hour. Then observe the outside of the container again. Describe it.

    _____

    _____

4. Draw and label diagrams of what happened.

 Next Question

Have an adult help you look behind a refrigerator. What similarities do you see between the back of the refrigerator and the experiment?

 Notebook Reflection

What do you think happened? Where did the water come from? What could make more water appear on the sides of the container?

Can I Build a Mini-World?

Name _____

What You Need:
- Empty 2-liter clear plastic bottle
- gravel
- potting soil
- small plants (boxwood, baby tears, *T. pallida*)
- mini-beasts (see page 77)
- potato cuttings
- scissors
- clear packing tape

What To Do:

1. Start by cutting off the top of your bottle. Set the top aside.

2. Layer the bottom of the bottle with some gravel and then 4 cm of soil. Dig two small holes in the soil and place a plant in each hole, patting the soil down around it. Sprinkle 100mL of water into the bottle. Add the potato cuttings and a few of your mini-beasts.

3. Replace the top of your bottle and attach it in place with packing tape. Make sure the bottle cap is screwed on top. You have built a mini-world. Set your mini-world on a windowsill where it will receive some sunlight. Make sure it will not be in direct sunlight all day long.

4. If drops of water form on the insides of the bottle and don't go away after a few days, unscrew the bottle top for fifteen minutes to release some moisture.

5. Every day, observe your mini-world. Describe what you see and any changes that happen inside it. Be sure to write down where your mini-beasts are and what they are doing. Can they be found in the same place every day? Why or why not?

Can I Build a Mini-World? *(cont.)*

What To Do: *(cont.)*

6. Draw your mini-world over four days. What changes? What doesn't? Be sure to label these in your drawings.

Next Question

How could you design a bigger, better mini-world? Draw your ideas on paper. Be sure to label the parts.

Notebook Reflection

Describe how your mini-world works. Use words and pictures.

What Is Wind?

Name _____

What You Need: • this lab sheet

What To Do:

1. Think about how you can "see" wind in the real world, and how it is shown in illustrations and in cartoons. Draw the wind.

What To Do: *(cont.)*

2. Go outside. Use all your senses to find situations where wind is having an effect. List all the situations you find in five minutes.

_____

_____

_____

_____

_____

_____

_____

Next Question

Compare your list with other students' lists. Compile a class list.

Notebook Reflection

List situations where the wind is useful, such as drying clothes on a clothesline. Then list situations where it is a nuissance, such as blowing trash around.

How Can I Measure the Wind?

Name _____

 What You Need:
- ruler
- string
- tape
- scissors
- five pieces of materials of different weight

 What To Do:

1. Use very small pieces of tape to stick each piece of material to a piece of string.

2. Tie the strings along the ruler, evenly spaced apart.

3. Take your wind gauge outside.

4. Hold the ruler across the wind. Keep it level, still, and away from your body.

5. Observe which materials move and how far they move. Work out a way to record these results in the space below.

? Next Question

Repeat the activity in other places to see if there are differences.

 Notebook Reflection

Why did different materials show how strong the wind was?

How Can I Measure the Wind Better?

Name _____

What You Need:
- ruler
- cardstock
- 30 cm (1 ft.) of string
- half a ping-pong ball
- tape
- scissors

What To Do:

1. Cut a semi-circle out of the card.

2. Use a small piece of tape to stick the end of the string to the inside of the ping pong ball.

3. Tape the other end of the string to the center of the semi-circle.

4. Attach the semi-circle along the end of a ruler.

5. Take your wind gauge outside.

6. Hold the ruler, pointing the semi-circle into the wind. Keep it level, still, and away from your body.

7. See how far the Ping Pong ball moves. Work out a way to record these results in the space below.

 Next Question

Repeat the activity in other places to see if there are differences.

Notebook Reflection

Describe how the experiment measured the wind.

Geology

This chapter provides activities that address McREL Science Standard 2.

Student understands Earth's composition and structure.

Knows how features on the Earth's surface are constantly changed by a combination of slow and rapid processes (e.g., slow processes, such as weathering, erosion, transport, and deposition of sediment caused by waves, wind, water, and ice; rapid processes, such as landslides, volcanic eruptions, and earthquakes)	*How Does Erosion Work?* (page 28) *What Happens to Frozen Clay?* (page 30) *How Do Stalactites and Stalagmites Form?* (see Teacher CD)
Knows that smaller rocks come from the breakage and weathering of larger rocks and bedrock	*What Is Inside Rocks?* (page 32) *How Are Sedimentary Rocks Formed?* (see Teacher CD)
Knows that rock is composed of different combinations of minerals	*What Happens to Chalk in Vinegar?* (page 34) *How Are Metamorphic Rocks Formed?* (see Teacher CD)
Knows the composition and properties of soils (e.g., components of soil such as weathered rock, living organisms, products of plants and animals; properties of soil such as color, texture, capacity to retain water, ability to support plant growth)	*What Is Soil Made Of?* (page 36) *What Are Different Soils Made Of?* (page 38) *Does Detergent Destroy Dirt?* (page 40) *Can I Take Soil Apart?* (page 42)
Knows that fossils provide evidence about the plants and animals that lived long ago and the nature of the environment at that time	*How Are Fossils Made?* (page 115) *What Is Amber?* (page 117)

How to Teach Geology

Is Soil Made from Dinosaur Droppings?

We live on a rocky planet. Wherever we are, even in the middle of the ocean, there are rocks beneath our feet. These rocks were formed as Earth began to cool.

That cooling process is far from over. Under the hard, cold crust of Earth, the mantle and core of the planet are still intensely hot. They are so hot that molten rock periodically bursts through the crust as volcanoes.

Much of the rock on Earth's surface was formed from this original material, the so-called igneous rocks. But some have been eroded, transported, and laid down in layers of sediment (sedimentary rocks). Some of these have been subjected to intense heat and pressure and have changed or metamorphosed (metamorphic rocks).

Rocks are constantly being broken down. The final product of this breakdown is soil or "earth." Unlike the student who guessed that earth was made of dinosaur droppings, we know that soil is a rich, complex material.

Beneath Our Feet

Earth is like a giant soft-boiled egg. Earth's core—the yolk of the egg—is incredibly hot and liquid. Earth's mantle—the white of the egg—surrounds it and is also hot and liquid. It breaks out in places as volcanoes.

Earth's crust—the shell of the egg—is cold and hard. It is made from solid rock. Wherever you are on Earth, even if you are on a ship in the middle of the sea, there is rock beneath you. You are on solid ground.

Just a minute. The school field isn't rock, nor is the park or the garden. That's because the rock is covered with a layer of earth or soil. If you dig down through this soil, you will find rock under it. Everywhere.

Plate Tectonics

About 200 million years ago, the landmasses of Earth were together as one supercontinent. This single landmass was called Pangea. We also know that the hot, molten magma under the surface of the crust pushed the lands apart. And this motion continues today!

The mid-ocean ridge is a huge underwater mountain range. It has a large crack running down its center. That crack is in Earth's crust. It allows molten magma to seep up. When magma reaches the surface, it is called lava. The lava cools and forms new rock on the ocean floor.

Molten magma rises to the surface through cracks in Earth's crust. This makes new crust. Does that mean there is more crust on the surface of Earth now than in the past? No. Geologists had a theory. If Earth oozed molten magma in one place, then it must reabsorb crust somewhere else.

Sure enough, studies began to show that the Atlantic Ocean floor is expanding. But the Pacific Ocean floor is shrinking. It was found that the Pacific Ocean floor dives down into deep trenches under continents. These trenches are called subduction zones. The expanding and shrinking ocean floors are an example of how Earth is really a recycler. Rocks are created and later recycled.

There are two basic types of plates on Earth. Oceanic plates are under the ocean water. Continental plates make up the continents. Plates have three main types of boundaries, or edges. They are divergent, convergent, and transform.

- Divergent boundaries are where two plates move away from each other.

- Convergent boundaries are where two plates crash into each other.

- Transform boundaries are where two plates slide past each other.

Each boundary behaves in a different way. The different boundaries can be found all over the world. The boundaries also make land features such as mountains and valleys.

Divergent Boundaries

Iceland is a tiny island made from the divergent boundary of the mid-ocean ridge. Two plates are moving away from each other very slowly. They move at a rate of two to four centimeters per year.

Volcanoes are common on the island nation of Iceland. The movement of the plates causes magma to burst up and through Earth's crust. This action forms volcanoes. The cooled material from the volcanic eruptions formed the island.

Convergent Boundaries

Plates can form convergent boundaries in one of three ways. Each type of convergent boundary has its own results.

An ocean-ocean collision happens between two ocean plates. Right now, such a collision is causing the Mariana Trench. The fast-moving Pacific Plate is crashing into the Philippine Plate. As the Pacific Plate dives into Earth's mantle, it is melted. This causes earthquakes and volcanoes. The Mariana Islands were made in this way.

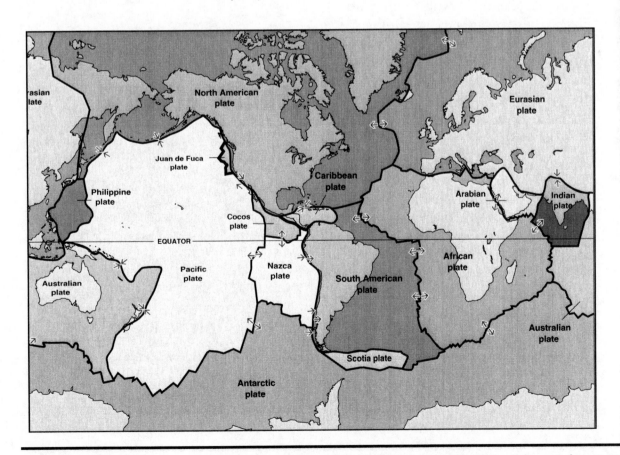

An ocean-continental collision is happening in South America right now. An oceanic plate is being subducted under a continental plate. This is happening near Peru and Chile. That is why earthquakes and volcanoes are very common in this area of the world.

In a continent-continent collision, two plates collide head-on. They "fight it out" before one plate finally subducts under the other. A lot of material builds up as it is scraped off one plate before it subducts. The Himalayas are the highest mountains in the world. They are the result of a collision that started about 50 million years ago. The Indian and Eurasian continental plates crashed together to form the very tall mountain range.

Transform Boundaries

The San Andreas fault in California is a transform boundary. It falls between the Pacific Plate and the North American Plate. These two plates are sliding past each other instead of colliding into each other. This sliding motion has caused major earthquakes in California all along the state. Most transform boundaries are found in the ocean, but the San Andreas fault is on land.

Where Soil Comes From

The weather transforms rocks. Remember we talked about the fact that water expands when it freezes? Well, even the strongest rock can be split by the "ice wedge"—water entering cracks in the rock, freezing, expanding, and splitting the rock apart. Smaller rocks are acted on by wind and rain, the sea, or plant or animal action. Finally, they break down to tiny particles which, mixed with organic matter from plants or animals, make up our soil. Soil is important to

plant growth, of course. And plant roots are important for securing the soil against weathering.

A Soil Profile

We are always digging up the ground. We dig holes to build houses and roads and to lay pipes and cables. If there is some digging near you, you might be able to visit it with a class or a group. Stand somewhere safe. Look into the hole that has been dug. You will see the soil profile.

- Topsoil: dark, rich, and full of rotting plants
- Subsoil: different in color; tightly-packed soil
- Rocky soil: a layer of rock that is breaking down to become soil
- Bedrock: this is the rock beneath the soil

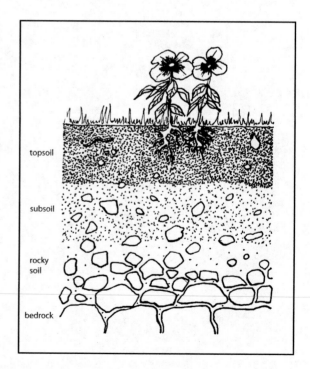

From Rock to Soil

But where does all this soil come from?

Rock is hard, but when the sun shines on it in the day, it swells up. When it is cold at night, it shrinks away. All this swelling and shrinking causes bits to break off. In the middle of winter, cracks fill up with water. The water freezes and the ice begins to push the rock apart. The ice splits the rock open. The river that sweeps past it bangs rocks against it, knocking off chips of rock.

Eventually, the rock crumbles to stone. The stones are rubbed and banged together by the river. The stones become gravel, then grains of sand, and then a fine powder. The powder becomes mixed with bits of rotting plants, living bacteria, tiny fungi that live off the rotting plants, trapped air, and water. The rock becomes soil.

Fascinating Fossils

Fossils are evidence of past life. They are the remains or imprints of living things from long ago. They can be leaf prints, footprints, shell prints, or skeleton prints. The waste from living things can even become fossils!

Fossils are made in different ways. They can be made when a living thing dies and becomes buried by sediments, such as ash from a volcano, mud, sand, or silt. They can be frozen in ice. They can be mummies, too. Some fossils have been buried in tar for thousands of years.

Most fossils are made when the soft parts of a living thing decay. The hard parts are turned into something like rock. The minerals in the sediments seep into the hard parts of the living thing. They become preserved as fossils. Other fossils are made when the whole living thing is frozen or mummified. Then, the soft parts are included, too.

Fossils are more likely to be made when a living thing dies near a body of water than on dry land. Near water, it is likely to be quickly buried. Over thousands of years, the sediments settle into layers that become sedimentary rock. Fossils are often found in sedimentary rock.

How Does Erosion Work?

Name _____

What You Need:
- newspaper
- two trays
- plastic jug with spout
- water
- block
- three different soil samples

What To Do:

1. Cover your table with newspaper.

2. Put soil 4 cm (2 in.) deep in one tray. Pat the soil down firmly so that it is level.

3. Put one side of the soil tray on a block so that it is on a slope. Put the empty tray under the end of the soil tray. This tray will catch the water.

4. Carefully pour a small stream of water into the top of the soil tray. The water should run down the soil.

5. When water reaches the bottom of the tray, stop pouring and check if the soil is moving. Draw and label a diagram in the box below.

How Does Erosion Work? *(cont.)*

What To Do: *(cont.)*

6. Pour more water into the tray until you notice another change. Then stop to draw and label a diagram in the box below.

 Next Question

Repeat the activity, but think of a way to change the setup. How would more or less soil, water, or slope change the results?

 Notebook Reflection

Describe erosion that you have seen outside the classroom. Where was it? What caused it? Were people trying to stop it? How?

What Happens to Frozen Clay?

Name _____

What You Need:
- clay
- plastic wrap
- water
- freezer

What To Do:

1. Divide the clay into two lumps.

2. Moisten the clay with water and roll it into two balls of the same size.

3. Wrap each ball in plastic wrap.

4. Leave one clay ball at room temperature. Place the other ball in a freezer. Leave overnight.

5. Predict what will happen to each ball.

_____

_____

_____

6. The next day, unwrap both balls and compare them. Draw what you see.

What Happens to Frozen Clay? *(cont.)*

What To Do: *(cont.)*

7. List the similarities and differences between the two balls.

_____

_____

_____

_____

_____

8. Was your prediction accurate?

_____

_____

_____

 **Next Question**

Predict what will happen if you put the ball of clay back into the freezer for another night. Then find out. Were you right?

 Notebook Reflection

Describe the steps you took to make a prediction, test it, and find out if you were right. How is this like what a scientist does?

What Is Inside Rocks?

Name _____

What You Need:
- small rock or pebble
- fabric square
- plastic bag
- hammer
- magnifying glass
- coarse sand
- gravel

What To Do:

1. Wrap the pebble in the fabric square. Put the fabric square inside the plastic bag.

2. Put the plastic bag on the concrete outside. Ask an adult to hit it with the hammer.

3. Unwrap the fabric square. Use the magnifying glass to look at the pebble pieces. Draw what you see:

What Is Inside Rocks? *(cont.)*

What To Do: *(cont.)*

4. Compare the pebble pieces to the sand and gravel. Draw and write about what you see:

Next Question

Repeat steps 1–3 with different pebbles. Are they the same inside, or different?

Notebook Reflection

How do you think the different pieces inside the pebbles got there? Draw and write your ideas.

What Happens to Chalk in Vinegar?

Name _____

What You Need:
- three clear plastic cups
- lemon juice
- vinegar
- water
- three pieces of chalk

What To Do:

1. Fill each cup halfway: one with lemon juice, one with vinegar, and one with water.

2. Place one pice of chalk in each cup.

3. Leave the cups in a safe place.

4. Make a prediction. What will happen in the different cups?

_____

_____

_____

_____

_____

_____

5. Observe the cups each day for three days. Draw and label diagrams to record what you see.

What Happens to Chalk in Vinegar? *(cont.)*

What To Do: *(cont.)*

Next Question

Research acid rain in the library or on the Internet. How is it similar to the experiment? How is it different?

Notebook Reflection

What happened to the chalks in the different liquids? What were the similarities? What were the differences?

What Is Soil Made Of?

Name _____

What You Need:
- soil sample
- graduated sieves
- scales
- containers

What To Do:

1. Collect 250 grams (8 oz.) of soil in a container.

2. Sift the soil through the largest sieve. Place whatever does not fit through the sieve into a container.

3. Repeat for each of the other sieves, in order from the largest to the smallest.

4. When you have finished sifting, observe what is left in each container.

Sieve 1	Sieve 2	Sieve 3	Sieve 4

What Is Soil Made Of? *(cont.)*

What To Do: *(cont.)*

5. Weigh each container (be sure to subtract the weight of the empty container).

sieve 1: _____

sieve 2: _____

sieve 3: _____

sieve 4: _____

total weight: _____

6. You started with 250 grams. Did the total weight change? _____

 **Next Question**

Compare your weights with other students. How similar were they?

 Notebook Reflection

Make some observations about soil based on the experiment.

What Are Different Soils Made Of?

Name _____

What You Need:
- measuring cup
- two different soil samples
- two clear plastic jars with lids
- water

What To Do:

1. Place 120 mL (1/2 c.) of one soil sample in a jar. Label it Sample A.

2. Fill the jar with water and secure the lid.

3. Repeat with the second soil sample in the second jar. Label it Sample B.

4. Shake the jars vigorously for one minute.

5. Leave the jars to stand for three days.

6. Observe the jars each day. Draw and label diagrams to record what you see.

Sample A, Day 1	Sample A, Day 2	Sample A, Day 3

Sample B, Day 1	Sample B, Day 2	Sample B, Day 3

What Are Different Soils Made Of? *(cont.)*

What To Do: *(cont.)*

7. Compare how Sample A looks after three days with how the soil sample looked before you mixed it with water. What changed? What stayed the same?

_____

_____

_____

8. Repeat step #7 for Sample B.

_____

_____

_____

9. What similarities and differences do you notice between Sample A and Sample B?

_____

_____

_____

Where did the soil samples come from? How could you test if their location had any

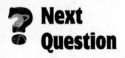

Next Question

affect on your results?

What might explain the similarities and differences that you found between the two soil samples?

Notebook Reflection

Does Detergent Destroy Dirt?

Name _____

What You Need:

- three plastic jars with lids
- three different samples of soil
- detergent
- water
- measuring cup

What To Do:

1. Fill one jar with water halfway. Add 5 mL (1 tsp) of detergent.

2. Sprinkle one type of soil into the jar until it is almost full. Leave a little space for air.

3. Seal the jar and label it with the type of soil.

4. Repeat for the other two jars with the other two soil samples

5. Shake all three jars vigorously for one minute.

6. When the contents are well mixed, put the jars on a flat surface. Leave them to settle.

7. Check them every twenty minutes. Draw what you see.

Does Detergent Destroy Dirt? *(cont.)*

What To Do: *(cont.)*

7. Draw what you see *(cont.)*

Next Question

Go outside and find some damp soil. Dig a hole with straight sides. Compare the sides of the hole with one of your jars. Are they similar or different? How?

Notebook Reflection

What do you think caused the differences between the different soil samples?

Can I Take Soil Apart?

Name _____

What You Need:
- cup of soil
- magnifying glass
- tweezers
- spoons
- toothpicks
- small containers
- white paper towels

What To Do:

1. Place two layers of paper towels on the table. Carefully spread your soil on the paper towel.

2. Use your magnifying glass to look for things that are moving.

3. Use a spoon to capture any mini-beasts. Put each one in a specimen container. Draw them:

4. Use your magnifying glass, tweezers, and toothpicks to separate the dead and decaying parts of the soil into piles.

Can I Take Soil Apart? *(cont.)*

What To Do: *(cont.)*

5. Look for things you can identify, such as skeletons, sticks, leaves, flower parts, and seeds. Draw them and make a tally in the space below:

6. Return your creatures to the soil. Help your teacher put the soil back where it came from.

7. Examine your paper towel. Is there any change?

_____

_____

 **Next Question**

Compare the things that you found with other students. What did you find out about the things that make up soil?

 Notebook Reflection

What do you think the most fertile soil is made of?

Astronomy

This chapter provides activities that address McREL Science Standard 3.

Student understands the composition and structure of the universe and the Earth's place in it.

Knows that night and day are caused by the Earth's rotation on its axis	*When Does the Sun Rise?* (page 49) *Why Does the Sun Rise and Set?* (page 50) *Where Does the Sun Go Each Day?* (page 52) *What Makes Night and Day?* (page 53)
Knows that the Earth is one of several planets that orbit the Sun and that the moon orbits the Earth	*What Is an Orrery?* (page 55)
Knows that the patterns of stars in the sky stay the same, although they appear to slowly move from east to west across the sky nightly and different stars can be seen in different seasons	*How do the Stars and Planets Move?* (page 58)
Knows that planets look like stars, but over time they appear to wander among the constellations	*How do the Stars and Planets Move?* (page 58)
Knows that astronomical objects in space are massive in size and are separated from one another by vast distances (e.g., many stars are more massive than our Sun but so distant they look like points of light)	*What is an Orrery?* (page 55)
Knows that telescopes magnify distant objects in the sky (e.g., the moon, planets) and dramatically increase the number of stars we can see	*How Do You Build a Telescope?* (page 62)

How to Teach Astronomy

Astronomy: It's a Big Subject

For many reasons, teaching about Earth in space is not easy. Children come to school with their own ideas about space, and some of those ideas are very difficult to dislodge.

They may believe, for example, that the Sun moves and Earth stands still. Given that the Sun apparently moves across the sky, this is understandable. Although the idea was questioned by Copernicus and later disproved by Galileo, the movement of the Sun was accepted science until the fifteenth century. This reflects our own observation, of course. Other commonly-held incorrect ideas include the theory that the Moon covers the Sun at night; that the shadow of Earth is what causes the apparent change in the shape of the Moon; and that the Sun is slightly further away from Earth in the winter (when in fact the opposite is true during winter in the northern hemisphere).

Three Important Concepts

Where Earth, Sun, and Moon are concerned, there are three important concepts to tackle. With these understood, the relationships of Earth, Sun, and Moon become clear.

1 Size

Earth, Sun, and Moon are all spherical—a function of the force of gravity, which pulls all matter toward the center of an object. Since the heavenly bodies are subject to their own force of gravity, they are all pulled towards their middles, and so tend to be ball-shaped. Very small objects in space don't have this large gravity force and so remain irregular in shape.

The heavenly bodies are subject to other gravity forces. The Sun's gravity keeps Earth and all the other planets in orbit. Earth's gravity keeps the Moon in orbit.

Because books often need to fit all three into a small picture, students have little idea of their relative sizes. You could fit a million Earths into the Sun. The differences are literally astronomical.

	Circumference	Diameter
Sun	4,370,880 km	1,392,000 km
Earth	40,076 km	12,756 km
Moon	10,915 km	3,476 km

2 Distance

If you model the Sun with a beach ball, Earth is about the size of a pea and the Moon the size of a peppercorn. Then the beach ball and pea would be placed 40 meters apart to approximate scale. In reality, Earth is about 152 million km from the Sun.

The Sun and the Moon appear to be the same size in the sky. The Sun is much further away, so although it is much bigger than the Moon, both look the same size. In the same way that you can cover a distant mountain with your thumbnail, so—rarely—the Moon covers the Sun, blotting it out completely. This event is called a solar eclipse.

3 Movement

The Sun is actually moving and spinning, together with the whole Solar System and the galaxy. For the sake of simplicity, let's imagine it is still. Earth orbits the Sun and spins as it does so. Both orbit and spin are counter-clockwise viewed from above. The orbit gives us our year; the spin gives us day and night.

Fascinating Fact

Earth spins at more than 1,600 km an hour. It also travels around the Sun at over 100,000 km an hour. We don't sense this movement. For us, Earth feels as though it is standing still.

Day and Night

Earth spins on its axis. Every 24 hours, it makes one complete rotation. It rotates counter-clockwise, seen from above. We call this complete turn a day. Part of Earth is always facing the Sun. This part is in daylight. Part will be facing away from the Sun. For this part of Earth, it is nighttime. As Earth spins, each part of Earth moves from light to dark and back to light again—from day to night, and back to day. From Earth, it looks as though the Sun is moving across the sky. However, it is Earth that is turning while the Sun stands still.

The Moon

The Moon is orbiting us. Since it always has its face turned towards us, the back of the Moon (incorrectly called the "dark" side) is constantly away from us. For this to happen, the Moon has to spin as well as orbit. Rotation and orbit are synchronized, so as it moves around Earth, the Moon turns to keep the same side facing Earth.

The Moon's orbit is not in the plane of the other planets. Since it bobs up and down, it can appear in many places in the sky (and during both day and night, though it is blotted out by the Sun's brightness as often as not).

The Moon is not a light source. It reflects the Sun's light. Because the Moon orbits around Earth through the month, it presents different sides to the Sun. When we on Earth can see all of the sunlit side, we call this a full Moon. When we can only see a little bit of the sunlit side, we call it a crescent, and so on.

The Seasons

Earth is going around the Sun. The time it takes to complete a full orbit—365 and a quarter days—we call a year.

Earth's axis is at a slight angle to the Sun: 23.5° to be exact. This angle stays the same as Earth orbits the Sun. Each pole spends some of the year leaning towards the Sun and in strong sunlight. This is summer in that hemisphere. It spends some of the year leaning away from the Sun, and then it will be winter there.

Planets in the Solar System

There are eight known planets orbiting the Sun. They are, in order from the Sun outwards:

- Mercury
- Venus
- Earth
- Mars
- Jupiter
- Saturn
- Uranus
- Neptune

Together, these planets make the Solar System. The planets vary greatly in size—and they aren't as close together as shown here!

How to Teach Astronomy (cont.)

Sizes and Distances

The planets vary greatly in size. Jupiter, the biggest, is 143,000 km across at the equator; Mercury, the smallest, less than 5,000 km across. If you model the planets using fruit, then Jupiter could be a watermelon and Mercury a blueberry, while Earth would be about the size of a strawberry.

The distances between the planets are enormous. If a house were your model of the Sun and you set off with your planet fruits, you would have to carry them away down the road to model the distances. The Mercury blueberry might not even be in the same town! Mercury orbits the Sun every 88 Earth days, but Neptune takes 165 Earth years to make a complete orbit.

It is even further to the nearest star (after our Sun). If Earth were a football, the next star would be on the other side of the planet!

Fascinating Fact

The Sun is a gigantic light source. Its surface is at a temperature of over 5,000° C. In the center, where nuclear reactions are turning hydrogen to helium, the temperature is 15 million° C. Although the Sun is around 150 million kilometers from us, its light can still harm your eyes if you look straight at it. Light from the Sun is reflected by the rocky Moon, which makes the Moon shine at night and gives us moonlight.

Fascinating Fact

Some parts of the Solar System are very hot—it is 465° C on Venus. Some are very cold—it is –220° C on Pluto.

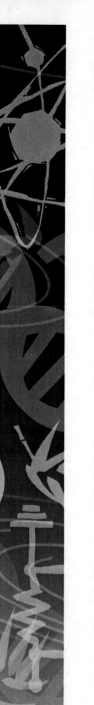

How to Teach Astronomy *(cont.)*

Many Moons

Earth is not the only planet with a moon. Mars has two moons: Phobos and Deimos. Jupiter has at least 16 moons, including Io and Europa. Saturn has about 23 moons, Uranus has 15, and Neptune has 8.

Other Citizens of the Solar System

In addition to the planets and their moons, the Solar System also has a number of other bodies within the orbits of the planets. Some of these also orbit the Sun, but others are merely drifting or orbit the planets, instead.

Dwarf planets like Pluto and Ceres are rocky bodies that have enough gravity to pull themselves into a sphere. Unlike planets, however, they are not large enough to clear their orbital path, and share the path with other objects. Ceres orbits within the asteroid belt; Pluto's orbit crosses Neptune's.

Comets have an icy head and a tail of dust and gas. They don't always trail their tail behind them. In fact, because the tail is always pointed away from the Sun, the tail goes first through half its orbit.

Asteroids are pieces of rubble. There is a belt of asteroid rubble between Mars and Jupiter.

Meteors are stony objects, some as small as a grain of sand. When they burn up in Earth's atmosphere, we call them shooting stars. Meteorites are larger. Some crash through the atmosphere and hit Earth.

Who's Orbiting Who?

Galileo said Earth orbited the Sun. He was prosecuted by the Inquisition because people didn't believe him. They believed the evidence of their own eyes. They saw the Sun rise, climb into the sky, sink, set, and dip below the horizon. They believed they saw a moving Sun. However, the Sun doesn't move around Earth. Earth moves around the Sun. To us on the moving Earth, this looks exactly the same as a moving Sun. No wonder people were confused!

Hazel on the Train

Here's an example to help illustrate this sometimes confusing concept.

Hazel was sitting in a train with her mother. She looked out of the window on her left. She could see into another train. She looked out of the window on her right. She could see the station. There were people standing on the platform. She looked back to her left. The windows of the train next to her were moving slowly past her window.

"That train is leaving the station!" she said to her mum.

"No, dear," said her mother. "That train is standing still. WE are leaving the station!"

Hazel looked to her right. Sure enough, they were passing the people on the platform. Her train was moving.

Hazel's train is like Earth, and the other train is like the Sun. Hazel's train is moving, and the other train is standing still.

When Does the Sun Rise?

Name _____

What You Need: • 5 consecutive days of the newspaper's weather sections

What To Do:

1. Make a class graph of the times that all the students in your class wake up in the morning.

2. Use the weather section of your newspapers. Find the time of sunrise and sunset each day. Record the data in the grid.

Date	Sunrise	Sunset

3. What season is it right now? _____

4. What do you notice about the sunrise times? _____

_____

5. What do you notice about the sunset times? _____

_____

6. Do you think that these times will be the same during the other seasons? Why or why not? _____

_____

Next Question

Perform the experiment during other seasons. What is the same? What is different?

Notebook Reflection

Think about the summer. Then think about the winter. Describe how long the days feel.

Why Does the Sun Rise and Set?

Name _____

What You Need:

- flashlight
- ball
- dark room

What To Do:

1. Make your classroom dark.

2. Hold up a ball to represent Earth. Mark a spot on it to represent where you are.

3. Use the flashlight to represent the Sun. Shine it onto one part of the ball. Then shine it onto different parts of the ball. Draw what you see.

4. How much of the ball is lit at any one time?

_____

5. Hold the flashlight steady so the light shines on the ball.

What To Do: *(cont.)*

6. Spin the ball around slowly. Do not move the flashlight. Watch the shadows and the spot you marked on the ball. Draw and write what you see.

 Next Question

Tilt the top of the ball away from the Sun. Spin it around. How does the light fall on the top of the ball differently than the bottom of the ball?

Notebook Reflection

Use words and drawings to describe how the Sun rises and sets. Explain how the experiment is similar and different from the actual Sun.

Where Does the Sun Go Each Day?

Name _____

What You Need:
- tall stick or pole
- short sticks or chalk
- ruler

What To Do:

1. Start this experiment in the morning. Find an open space. Put the stick or pole in the ground so that it stands vertically.

2. Use chalk to draw the shadow of the pole, or mark the end of the shadow with a short stick in the ground.

3. Repeat step #2 every hour.

4. Draw the pattern that the chalk or sticks create over the course of the day.

 Next Question

Perform the experiment at different times of the year. Compare the patterns the shadows create.

Notebook Reflection

Why does the shadow move? Why does the shadow not move in a perfect circle?

What Makes Night and Day?

Name _____

What You Need:
- ball
- small sticker or marker
- flashlight

What To Do:

1. Make the classroom dark.

2. Hold up a ball to represent Earth. Use the sticker or marker to mark where you are on Earth.

3. Use the flashlight to represent the Sun. Shine it onto one part of the ball. Then shine it onto different parts of the ball. Draw the ball, light, and shadows in the space below.

How much of the ball is lit at any one time? _____

What To Do: *(cont.)*

4. Hold the flashlight steady so the light shines on the ball. Spin the ball around slowly without moving the light. Watch the shadows and the spot you marked on the ball. Draw pictures of what you see. Use shading to show night and day.

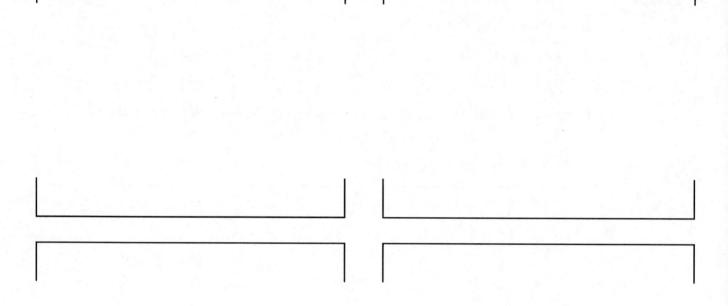

 Next Question

What happens if you spin Earth in a different way? How can you make some parts of Earth get sunlight the whole time?

Notebook Reflection

Describe the experiment in your science notebook. Be careful to record your observations. Use drawings as well as words.

What Is an Orrery?

Name _____

What You Need:
- your classmates
- this lab sheet

The class is going to make an orrery. An orrery is a model of the solar system that shows the orbits of the celestial bodies. Most orreries are made out of metal spheres, but you will use students, instead.

What To Do:

1. First, you will need to pick your celestial body. Taking turns, everyone in the classroom will pick a planet, moon, dwarf planet, asteroid, or ring from the list at the end of the lab. (Your teacher may have you cross out some of the asteroids before the class picks.)

   Once you have your celestial body, answer the following four questions:

   I am _____ .

   I am a _____ .

   I orbit _____ .

   I am _____AU from the Sun.

2. The solar system is very big, so you will need to be outside or in a large gymnasium. The Sun stands in the middle of the field or the room. The rest of the students will stand in their orbits around the Sun. Going down the list, each student should count a number of strides away from the Sun equal to their orbit in AU. (A stride is two steps.) If you orbit a planet, make sure you end up next to your planet! If there are enough asteroids, they can link hands in a circle around the Sun.

   Once you're in your orbit, fill out the following questions:

   From where I'm standing, the Sun is _____ .

   Number of other celestial bodies that are close to me: _____

What Is an Orrery? *(cont.)*

What To Do: *(cont.)*

3. Now it's time to put the orrery in motion. Look at the celestial body that you orbit. You are going to walk around them, always staying the same distance away. That may mean that you go way around them! Everyone will walk in a counter-clockwise direction (unless you're Triton; then you go clockwise!). Your teacher will tell you when to start and when to stop.

Once you've walked your orbit, fill out the following questions:

From where I'm standing, the Sun is _____ .

Number of other celestial bodies that are close to me: _____

The place where I started is _____ .

I went around my orbit _____ times.

I went around the Sun _____ times.

Compared to the other planets, my orbital path is _____ .

Draw your orbital path in the space below. Draw and label any other celestial bodies that will help make your path clearer.

Sun

What Is an Orrery? *(cont.)*

What To Do: *(cont.)*

4. Make three more observations about your own orbit or the orbit of another celestial body.

_____

_____

_____

_____

_____

Sun	**Asteroid Belt**	**Jupiter (5.2 AU)**	**Uranus (19.6 AU)**
Mercury (.4 AU)	**(2.75 AU)**	**Ganymede**	**Titania**
Venus (.7 AU)	**Ceres**	**Callisto**	**Oberon**
Earth (1 AU)	**Vesta**	**Europa**	**Umbriel**
Moon	**Pallas**	**Io**	**Ariel**
Mars (1.5 AU)	**Eros**	**Saturn (9.5 AU)**	**Miranda**
Phobos	**Fortuna**	**A Ring**	**Neptune (30 AU)**
Deimos	**Iris**	**B Ring**	**Triton (retrograde)**
	Leda	**C Ring**	**Pluto (39 AU)**
	Psyche	**D Ring**	**Charon**

 ### Next Question

Research and write a report on your celestial body. Be sure to include its orbit, composition, day, year, temperature, atmosphere (if any), and how it got its name. What does it orbit? Does anything orbit your celestial body?

 ### Notebook Reflection

Describe your experience as a part of the orrery. Imagine what an astronaut would see if he visited your celestial body. What would the Sun look like? Would the astronaut see moons or a planet or rings? Where would they be in the sky?

How Do the Stars and Planets Move?

Name _____

What You Need:
- copies of star map, frame, and triangles
- cardboard
- scissors or craft knife
- glue
- fine sandpaper

What To Do:

1. Paste the star map, frame, and triangles onto the cardboard, making sure there are no creases or bubbles. Place these on a table, bench, or floor with heavy books on top. Leave them to press for an hour or so.

2. Use sharp scissors or a craft knife to cut out the star map, frame, and triangles.

3. Glue the triangles onto the back corners of the frame. Let them dry.

4. Cut out a square of cardboard 20 cm (8 in.) on a side.

5. Use the sandpaper to smooth the edges of the star map and frame (when it's dry).

6. Fit the star map inside the triangles on the back of the frame. Part of the star map should show through the frame.

7. Place the square of cardboard behind the star map and use a very small bit of glue on each triangle to fix it in place. The star map should be able to spin inside the frame.

8. You've made a planisphere, or star atlas. You can use it to identify stars at night.

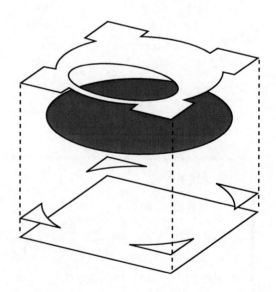

What To Do: *(cont.)*

9. Take your planisphere outside at night when you can see some stars. Spin the star map until the hour lines up with the date. Hold the planisphere over your head, pointing the "N" on the planisphere north. Can you spot stars from the planisphere in the sky? Write down the names of stars that you find.

_____   _____   _____

_____   _____   _____

_____   _____   _____

10. If you spend a long time finding stars, you'll have to spin the star map a little so the time always lines up with the date. Why do you think this is necessary?

_____

_____

_____

_____

Next Question

Using your library or the Internet, find the current locations of the planets. Their positions are usually listed by what constellation they can be found in. On a clear night, see how many of the planets you can find. Over time, the planets move across the sky. Why do you think this is?

Notebook Reflection

Describe your stargazing in your notebook. What was the first star you found? How did you find other stars? Did you find anything particularly difficult? Did you figure out some tricks to make finding stars easier?

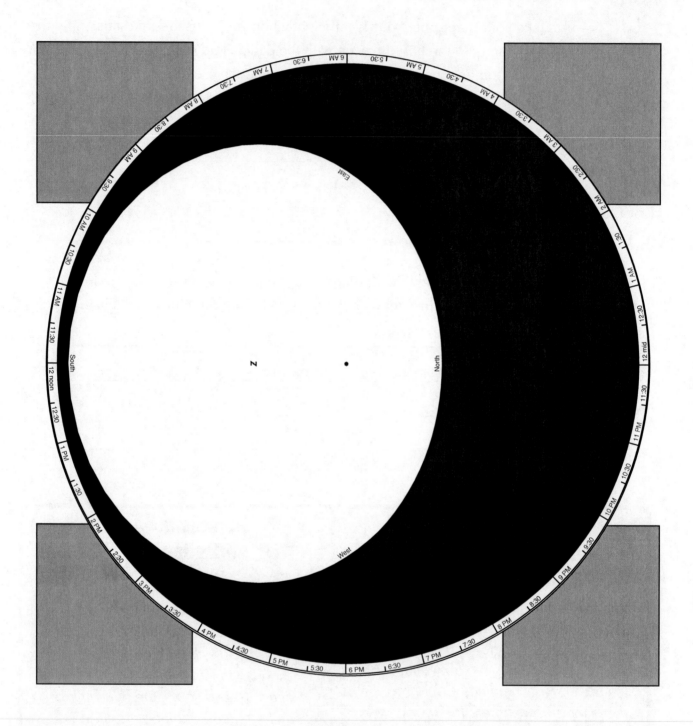

Teacher Note: This frame works best for classrooms at 45 degrees north latitude. Additional frames for 40°N and 50°N can be found on the Teacher Resource CD.

How Do the Stars and Planets Move? *(cont.)*

How Do You Build a Telescope?

Name _____

What You Need:
- weak convex lens (focal length 15 cm)
- posterboard
- foil or construction paper
- tape, stapler, glue
- pin

What To Do:

1. Roll a piece of posterboard into a tube that is the same width as the lens. Tape or staple the tube in place. Tape or glue the lens into one end of the tube. This is your objective.

2. Roll a second piece of posterboard into a tube that is slightly narrower. The second tube should be able to fit inside the first tube. Tape or staple the tube in place.

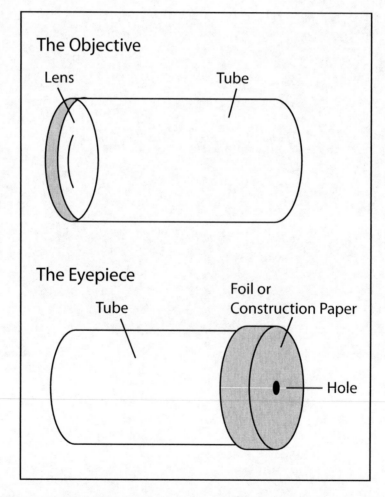

The Objective

Lens

Tube

The Eyepiece

Tube

Foil or Construction Paper

Hole

How Do You Build a Telescope? *(cont.)*

What To Do: *(cont.)*

3. Cover one end of the second tube with foil or construction paper. Use tape or glue to secure it in place. Use a pin to poke a small, circular hole in the center of the construction paper or foil. This is your eyepiece.

4. Put the two tubes together with the objective on one end and the eyepiece on the other. Point the lens end at a bright image outside, like a tree or building. Look through the eyepiece. Move the eyepiece tube back and forth in the objective tube to bring the image into focus.

5. What do you see? What happens when you make the telescope longer? What happens when you make it shorter? What do you see when you look through just one half of the telescope? Why do you think this happens?

_____

_____

_____

_____

_____

_____

_____

_____

How Do You Build a Telescope? *(cont.)*

What To Do: *(cont.)*

6. On a clear night when the moon is near full, go outside and look at the moon through your telescope. Draw what you see in the space below:

Next Question

Draw a diagram of your telescope on a piece of paper. Draw the path of light as it enters the telescope, bends through the lens, and through the eyepiece.

Notebook Reflection

Imagine you are the first person to view the moon through a telescope. Everyone else in the world believes the moon is a perfectly smooth sphere. Write down how you would describe what you have seen to someone else.

Heredity

This chapter provides activities that address McREL Science Standard 4.

Student understands the principles of heredity and related concepts.

Knows that reproduction is a characteristic of all living things and is essential to the continuation of a species	*Why Am I Who I Am?* (page 71)
Understands asexual and sexual reproduction (e.g., in asexual reproduction, all the genes come from a single parent; in sexual reproduction, an egg and sperm unite and half of the genes come from each parent, so the offspring is never identical to either of its parents; sexual reproduction allows for greater genetic diversity; asexual reproduction limits the spread of disadvantageous characteristics through a species)	*How Do Genes Pass Traits?* (page 69)
Knows that hereditary information is contained in genes (located in the chromosomes of each cell), each of which carries a single unit of information; an inherited trait of an individual can be determined by either one or many genes, and a single gene can influence more than one trait	*How Do Genes Pass Traits?* (page 69)
Knows that the characteristics of an organism can be described in terms of a combination of traits; some traits are inherited through the coding of genetic material and others result from environmental factors	*How Do Genes Pass Traits?* (page 69) *Why Am I Who I Am?* (page 71)

How to Teach Heredity

Students are growing and changing, illustrating how we all change as we mature and age. They may well have had experiences with birth and death through family or their pets; they may be beginning to understand the cyclical nature of life.

Reproduction is the process of making young. Each species reproduces its own kind. People make people. Dogs make dogs. Trees make trees. Reproduction is needed for species to survive.

Asexual Reproduction

There are two forms of reproduction. In asexual reproduction, something can reproduce all by itself. It does not need a partner. One parent cell divides. It forms two new cells. The cells are identical to the parent cell. Bacteria cells reproduce asexually. Most plants have the ability to reproduce asexually, too.

Sexual Reproduction

Sexual reproduction involves the combining of genetic material from both parents to produce a new individual. It happens with both plants and animals. Sometimes the product of the process doesn't even look alive. Some students believe that hens' eggs and seeds are not alive, though in changed circumstances either may produce new life—though not, of course, "breakfast eggs" which are not fertilized.

Research has shown that for many students, new life is formed from components or parts—new human babies manufactured "in a mommy's tummy" from bits, and chicks assembled from kits of legs, wings, head, and body floating around inside the egg.

It's just not like that. All life begins as a single cell—usually the result of combining the cells of two different parents. But there can be reproduction without fertilization—asexual reproduction and even cloning.

Sexual reproduction has the great advantage that it mixes the characteristics of parent organisms and gives them a big stir. The resulting offspring has characteristics from both parents.

Making a Baby

When animals reproduce sexually, they make special sex cells, each containing half a complete set of DNA. Fertilization is the process that combines these two cells to make a new one. The new cell will have a complete set of DNA.

Because the male cells—the sperm—need water to swim in, many animals reproduce in water. Amphibians like toads and frogs need to return to the water to breed. Land animals have developed internal fertilization. The male puts the sperm inside the female's body. Then the new animal develops in a mini-pond—the egg—or inside the mother in the womb. The egg, or the mother's womb, provides a food supply for the developing animal. Eggs are laid and eventually hatch. Mammals are born when the young animal is pushed from the mother's body.

Do Plants Have Babies?

While many students can accept that animals reproduce sexually, very few believe that plants reproduce sexually, perhaps because they may equate sexual reproduction with copulation.

How Plants Reproduce

Most green plants have special structures called flowers. Flowers are the reproductive parts of the plant. Flowers are fine examples of biodiversity. There is a huge range of types, in many colors, patterns, and shapes. But they all have the same aim—the continuation of the species.

The geranium is a plant with soft, furry leaves. Often, the flowers are red or pink. You can make new plants from an old one. Carefully break off a side branch from the main stem by pulling it downwards. Press your cutting into a small pot of compost or soil. Water it regularly. It will grow roots and eventually become a plant exactly like its parent. You have created a clone!

Life follows a distinct cycle, with birth, growth, and reproductive phases—always ending in death. Understandably, animal metamorphosis—the spectacular life-cycle in which animals undergo huge changes, such as caterpillar to butterfly or tadpole to frog—catches the imagination. But most animals produce young that resemble the adult—even those that go through partial metamorphosis—a "nymph" stage.

Plant reproduction can be equally interesting, especially if—like many primary-aged students—you believe that seeds grow in packets at the gardening store!

Male and female plant cells must be brought together for seeds to form. This process is called pollination. The male stamens produce pollen in their anthers. The pollen is carried to another flower by the wind or by insects. When the pollen grain reaches the stigma of another flower, it grows a pollen tube down to the female ovule. The ovule is fertilized and forms a seed. The ovary becomes a fruit: the container of the seed.

Green plants carry flowers, whose sole purpose in life is to ensure that their ovum is fertilized by pollen from another plant, either wind-blown or delivered by insects. Flowering plants produce seeds which are carried away, ensuring that when the new plants grow, they do not compete with their parents. The seeds are commonly carried on (strawberry) or inside (apple) fruits. These fruits are often intended to be eaten–which is good news for us and for other animals. The seeds may be discarded, or they may pass through the eater to reach the ground and germinate. Seeds of other fruits—like the tufts of the dandelion—are carried on the wind.

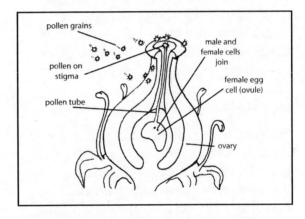

What Is a Chromosome?

How can we understand why humans are the way we are? We have to look at our cells. We must look at a material found in the center of our cells. This material is our chromosomes.

Chromosomes are found in each of our cells. We have 23 pairs of chromosomes. That means each cell has 46 in all. Chromosomes are made up of alleles. Each one has more than 2,000 alleles along its length. Alleles are instructions for cells.

How to Teach Heredity *(cont.)*

Because chromosomes come in pairs, alleles come in pairs, too. Each cell has two sets of instructions for everything. Two paired alleles work together to make a gene.

A zebra's genes give it stripes. A bird's genes give it wings. Our genes give us fingers and everything else that makes us human. Stripes, wings, and fingers are all traits. Those traits start in the cells. Each cell follows its gene's instructions on how to develop and work. All the cells work together to make stripes, wings, or fingers.

Remember how each cell has two sets of instructions for everything? A full set of chromosomes has 23 pairs. Each pair has one chromosome from the mother and one from the father. If the father were blonde and the mother were blonde, the chromosomes they gave the baby would have blonde alleles. Then the baby would be blonde.

Sometimes the mother and father do not have the same alleles. Then the baby gets chromosomes with different alleles on them. The father's chromosome may have the attached earlobe allele. The mother's chromosome may have the unattached earlobe allele. The baby's cells follow both sets of instructions at the same time. What kind of earlobes will the baby have?

Some alleles are dominant. Others are recessive. If a dominant allele is present, that trait will show up. So, if two dominant alleles are present, the dominant trait will show up. When one dominant and one recessive allele are present, the dominant allele will still show up. However, if two recessive alleles are present, the recessive trait will show up.

Alleles are passed down over generations. A recessive allele can "hide" behind dominant alleles for many generations before popping up and surprising the whole family with blue eyes or red hair.

How Do Genes Pass Traits?

Name _____

What You Need:
- white frosting
- strips of paper
- food coloring (red, blue, yellow, green)
- small paper cups
- stir sticks

What To Do:

1. Take two strips of paper. Down each strip of paper, draw three boxes. These will be the chromosomes of your first organism.

2. Fill each box with one of any of these letters: R, G, B, Y. These are your organism's alleles.

3. Put a small dollop of frosting in a paper cup. Label your cup Generation One.

4. Put the strips of paper down in front of you. For each letter, add one drop of food coloring to your frosting. Use the color that starts with that letter.

5. Stir up your frosting. Describe the color you get.

_____

_____

_____

6. Find a partner. Describe the color that they got in their cup.

_____

_____

_____

What To Do: *(cont.)*

7. Trade one chromosome with your partner. Get a new cup with a dollop of frosting. Label this cup Generation Two.

8. Repeat steps #4 and #5 with your new cup. Describe the color you get now.

_____

_____

_____

9. How is the color of Generation Two the same and different from its "parents" in Generation One?

_____

_____

_____

 **Next Question**

Repeat the experiment for further generations, trading chromosomes with different students. Do you notice some patterns emerge?

 Notebook Reflection

Explain how the experiment is similar to the chromosomes and alleles in real organisms. Use an example from your family.

Why Am I Who I Am?

Name _____

What You Need:
- old magazines to cut out pictures
- large pieces of construction paper
- glue
- scissors

What To Do:

1. Raise your hand to answer "yes" to the questions your teacher asks. Count how many hands are in the air for each question.

Are you...	a person?	a boy?	a girl?
Do you like...	ice cream?	basketball?	school?
Do you have...	brown hair?	red hair?	blond hair?
Is your hair...	straight?	wavy?	curly?
Do you have...	long hair?	short hair?	no hair?

2. When the questions were answered, what similarities did you notice? What differences did you notice? _____

3. Which answers are genetic (or inherited from your parents)?

_____

4. Which answers are matters of choice (not inherited from your parents)?

_____

5. Select a living thing to explore similarities and differences. You might want to pick flowers, cats, dogs, fish, or even people. Cut out pictures from the magazines that fit the category you picked and glue the pictures onto the construction paper.

6. Write a sentence explaining how the items are similar and how they are different.

 Next Question

Besides genetics, what else could influence how something looks or grows?

 Notebook Reflection

What would this world be like if everything looked the same—all dogs were the same breed, all flowers were the same shape and color, all cats were white?

Biology

This chapter provides activities that address McREL Science Standard 5.

Student understands the structure and function of cells and organisms.

Knows that plants and animals progress through life cycles of birth, growth and development, reproduction, and death; the details of these life cycles are different for different organisms	*What's in the Bran?* (page 78) *How Do Mealworms Live?* (page 80)
Knows that living organisms have distinct structures and body systems that serve specific functions in growth, survival, and reproduction (e.g., various body structures for walking, flying, or swimming)	*How Mini Is My Beast?* (page 81) *How Do Plants Grow?* (page 83) *How Does My Grass Grow?* (page 85) *How Can I Grow My Own Lunch?* (page 86) *How Are Seeds Different?* (page 88) *How Do My Hands Work?* (page 90) *How Many Bones Are in My Hand?* (page 92) *How Can I Dissolve a Cookie?* (page 93) *What Do Mini-Beasts Look Like Up Close?* (see Teacher CD)
Knows that the behavior of individual organisms is influenced by internal cues (e.g., hunger) and external cues (e.g., changes in the environment), and that humans and other organisms have senses that help them to detect these cues	*How Do Mini-Beasts Travel?* (page 108)

How to Teach Biology

Cell Theory

The foundation of modern biology is cell theory. Cell theory has three parts:

- All living things are made of cells.

- Cells are the smallest part of living things that are themselves alive.

- All cells come from other cells.

Cells are microscopic clumps of chemicals bound by membranes. Inside the cell, complex organic chemicals receive materials from outside of the cell, break those materials apart to release energy and nutrients, and then use that energy and nutrients to make new materials that the cell needs. The chemicals receive "instructions" from the cell's DNA—itself an incredible complex organic chemical. In fact, the instructions are passed along from the DNA to the rest of the cell through chemical reactions.

The vast majority of living things on planet Earth, both in number and by biomass, are organisms made up of one cell. The rest of the living world—and the part that we're most familiar with—consists of organisms made of more than one cell: plants, animals, and the occasional fungus.

Animals

Animals are multicellular heterotrophs. They are composed of more than one cell (multicellular), and they eat other organisms to survive (heterotroph).

The hardest part of any animal's life is staying alive! To do this animals need to:

- eat

- keep warm

- evade hunters

Food

Animals need food for energy. They release that energy by a cellular process called respiration. (It mustn't be forgotten that plants respire, too; they do not produce food as a selfless activity to support the animal kingdom.) Respiration and the release of energy from food require oxygen. Animals are unable to store oxygen. It is the need to regularly renew oxygen stores that leads them to breathe in different ways—through breathing tubes (insects); through gills (fish and young amphibians); through their skin and the lining of their mouths (frogs); or with lungs (reptiles, birds, and mammals).

This process releases the energy needed for life. Animals need to maintain this process to survive. This makes the finding and ingesting of food an imperative for every animal on Earth.

Heat

Living things function because of chemical reactions in their bodies. These chemical reactions run faster and more efficiently in warmer conditions. Their body temperature varies with their environment. Cold-blooded animals become less active in cold conditions—or may boost their body temperature by basking in the sun.

Mammals and birds maintain their body temperature as if they had an internal thermostat. Since these animals need to maintain these temperatures, they are affected by seasonal change. They may stay active throughout the cold conditions, evade them by going somewhere warmer (migration), or become inactive for weeks at a time (hibernation).

Run, Hide... or Fight Back.

Animals have a variety of ways of evading their predators. They might be able to outrun them—as in the case of the hare escaping the fox. But if they can't, then what other tricks do they have up their sleeves? One option is camouflage, by which the animal changes in some way to match its surroundings. Examples include the changing color of the chameleon and the stick insect who looks just like the twig she is sitting on.

Some animals need have no fear of enemies because they are so unpleasant-tasting, or poisonous, that they can be vividly-colored, advertising their unpleasantness. A bright red ladybird presumably tastes disgusting to a bird. Many spiders and scorpions have a deadly bite or sting, and some tarantulas are happy to stand back and fire irritating hairs at their enemies.

Perceiving the World

Animals need sense organs to find their way around. Putting the sense organs at the front or top of the body makes them more useful. If the animal is a secondary consumer—a predator or carnivore—the sense organs are likely to be forward-facing, enabling it to see its prey and to catch it efficiently. If the animal is a primary consumer, or herbivore, then its sense organs are likely to survey the surroundings more generally. It needs to be aware of predators and danger. Cats have eyes on the front of their heads; mice have them on the side. Cats have excellent, stereoscopic forward vision to catch mice; mice have good all-around vision to spot and avoid cats.

Fascinating Facts

What Is a Life-Cycle?

The process of birth, growth, reproduction, aging, and death is the animal's life-cycle.

Animals' longest-known life span

adult mayfly	3 days
mouse	3 years
guppy	5 years
large beetles	5–10 years
swallow	9 years
coyote	15 years
giant spider	20 years
toad	36 years
lobster	50 years
crocodile	60 years
sea anemone	70 years
elephant	77 years
blue whale	80 years
golden eagle	80 years
sturgeon	100 years
tortoise	100–150 years
human	113 years

Plants

Plants are multicellular autotrophs. They are composed of more than one cell (multicellular), and they produce their own food (autotroph).

Plants Are Alive!

Yes, plants are alive, too! Piaget first identified the stages that students move through in their understanding of "the life concept." His research suggests that at a young age, movement is equated with life. Things that appear to move by themselves—including rivers and the Sun—are deemed alive.

If that type of confusion seems improbable, consider the apple you are about to eat for your lunch. You may have difficulty in believing that it is alive—not the plant from which it came, but the apple itself. It respires using its own food source, excretes waste gases, and could reproduce, given the right conditions for its seeds. No wonder that, while all 8- to 11-year-olds appear to agree that plants grow, only 69 percent of them regard plants as living.

Animals clearly show the seven life processes, but plants—which may look dead at some times of the year—show them all, too.

1. Nutrition: Green plants can make their own food, but they need that food to grow and live.

2. Growth: Plants grow, sometimes very slowly. But a new seedling grows a lot faster than a human baby!

3. Reproduction: Plants can produce seeds or spores. Some plants reproduce by growing new plants from special stems or roots.

4. Respiration: Plants need oxygen to live, and they produce carbon dioxide. Fortunately for us, they produce a lot of oxygen, too!

5. Sensitivity: Plants are sensitive to their surroundings. Climbing bean plants sense a stick, and twine around it.

6. Excretion: Plants produce waste products—a little carbon dioxide and a lot of oxygen.

7. Movement: Plants move. Some move quite fast, like mimosa, the sensitive plant that closes its leaves when you touch it. Others move more slowly, like the dandelions that open for the Sun, and close at night.

Making Their Own Food

Green plants are the only living things able to make their own food. They combine water with carbon dioxide from the air and chlorophyll from the leaves to produce glucose (a type of sugar). This process needs light energy, usually from the Sun, and is called photosynthesis. Plants also need to absorb tiny quantities of mineral salts and other nutrients from the soil and we confuse this process by calling it "feeding" the plant. Plants don't feed—they are food producers and the first step in most food chains.

Don't forget that plants also respire, just like us. They don't breathe by mechanically drawing air into and expelling it from the body, but they use oxygen in their cells in the process that releases energy from stored foods. At night, they respire but do not photosynthesize. During the day, they are doing both. Fortunately for life on Earth, the amounts of oxygen plants use are exceeded by the amounts they produce.

How to Teach Biology *(cont.)*

Take a deep breath; here we go. To start with, photosynthesis takes place in two stages. In the first, sunlight is used to split water into oxygen and hydrogen. This depends upon the ability of a green pigment in plants called chlorophyll to split water molecules. The oxygen is now a waste product—which is a good thing for those of us who favor breathing.

Next, a reaction takes place which doesn't need light. It takes place in a billionth of a second. The hydrogen (actually split into bits by now) is used to convert carbon dioxide into carbohydrates—basic building blocks for sugars, starch, and a wide range of materials. One of these is cellulose, the material that plant cell walls are made from. As a result, the plant has food for activity and material for growth, both of which we can exploit by eating a cucumber sandwich.

Why Are Plants That Shape?

To make their food by photosynthesis, plants need to catch the light of the Sun. Their whole structure is aimed at collecting and using as much sunlight as possible.

They have a branching root system that can grip the soil. There is as much tree below the ground as above it (the roots of a tree are roughly the same size and extent as its canopy). They have a strong stem (sometimes a trunk) that can hold the leaves up high—and above the leaves of competitors—and a mathematically—precise leaf pattern.

If you want to see the effectiveness of the leaf pattern, stand under a tree on a sunny day. The leaves are laid out to ensure that even the lower ones make use of the light missed by those above them. The result is nearly complete coverage.

Fungi Are NOT Plants!

Fungi are either saprotrophs or parasites. Saprotrophs eat non-living matter. Parasites get their energy and nutrients from a host organism without killing it first. Fungi may be multicellular, in the case of mushrooms, or unicellular, in the case of yeast.

Fungi are not green—they cannot make their own food like plants. They produce spores, not seeds. Their structure can spread for miles under the ground.

Microorganisms

Most single-celled or unicellular organisms are presently grouped into three kingdoms: protoctista, bacteria, and archaea. However, this is a temporary classification solution at best. These three kingdoms represent more diversity of life than all the other kingdoms combined.

Students call microorganisms "bugs" or "germs." These names include small invertebrates, bacteria, and viruses. The names are associated with dirt, death, and disease. Students may think of microorganisms as things that walk about inside us, eating, breeding, and making us ill. Given the opportunity, they would probably exterminate all microorganisms, thus inadvertently bringing the world to a speedy end!

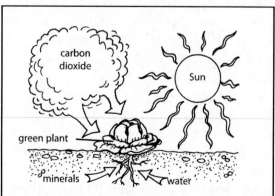

How to Teach Biology *(cont.)*

Few students are aware of the beneficial effects of microorganisms and have little idea of their importance in decay and recycling. They may not understand that we live surrounded by microorganisms of all sorts, and that we are dependent on them for our health and well-being.

It's difficult to teach about microorganisms because you're teaching about something that is invisible to the naked eye. It's very hard to envision a microscopic world of the size and complexity that exists. It is harder still to give students actual experiences of that world.

In promoting the benefits of microorganisms, point out that they are essential to making leavened bread, cheese, yogurt, vinegar, and many protein meat substitutes. They are essential to the production of many medicines and the breakdown of sewage.

Fascinating Facts
Algae

The term "algae" can mean any number of different organisms that have little to no relation to each other and very little in common. Everything from seaweed to cyanobacteria has been counted as an algae at one time or another, to the point that the term itself is problematic at best.

Mini-Beasts

Some of the most accessible animals available to students are "mini-beasts"—insects, pillbugs, centipedes, even earthworms. These fascinating creatures can give students an up-close look at the basic needs and structure of animal life. These animals do not fall into a neat category. They are not all insects, but include arachnids, annelids, and even crustaceans in the case of the pillbug. This text refers to these scientific gold mines as "mini-beasts" and includes a number of labs investigating their small and educational world.

What's in the Bran?

Name _____

What You Need:
- tub of natural bran and mealworms
- paintbrush
- plastic spoon
- ruler
- magnifying glass

What To Do:

1. Look carefully through the contents of the tub. Use a plastic spoon to turn things over. List the things you can see.

_____

_____

_____

2. Use the magnifying glass to look at two items. Measure them and draw enlarged diagrams.

_____

_____

_____

_____

_____

_____

_____

What To Do: *(cont.)*

3. Use the grid below to write a question about mealworms in each box.

	What	How	When	Why
can				
do/does				
is/are				
have				

? Next Question

What is the density of mealworms in the bran?

 **Notebook Reflection**

How do you think the things you saw are related?

How Do Mealworms Live?

Name _____

What You Need:
- tub of natural bran
- mealworms
- potato or carrot

What To Do:

1. Put a small piece of potato or carrot in the tub to provide moisture for the mealworms.

2. Write the date in the grid below and describe what you see in the tub.

3. Leave the tub in a warm, safe place with good ventilation.

4. Check the tub each week for six weeks. Record what you see.

Date:	
Date:	
Date:	
Date:	
Date:	
Date:	

 Next Question

Research another animal that goes through a metamorphosis.

 Notebook Reflection

Draw and label diagrams to show the four stages of mealworm metamorphosis.

How Mini Is My Beast?

Name _____

What You Need: • mini-beasts

Measuring Strip

What To Do:

1. Collect a variety of mini-beasts.

2. Choose one and write the type of mini-beast.

   Mini-beast 1: _____

3. Estimate its length. How many squares long is it?

   _____ squares

4. Place it on the measuring squares to check. Record the length you measure.

   _____ squares

5. Draw Mini-beast #1.

6. Repeat for two more mini-beasts.

   Mini-beast 2: _____

   Estimation:

   _____ squares

   Measurement:

   _____ squares

What To Do: *(cont.)*

 Draw Mini-beast #2.

Mini-beast 3: _____

Estimation:

_____ squares

Measurement:

_____ squares

Draw Mini-beast #3.

 Next Question

Who had the longest mini-beast in the class? The shortest? Make a graph that shows the results of the whole class.

 Notebook Reflection

Why do you think some mini-beasts are larger or smaller? Use words and drawings in your answer.

How Do Plants Grow?

Name _____

What You Need:
- 4 plastic cups
- paper towels
- ruler
- 4 types of beans (from seed packets)
- water
- measuring cup

What To Do:

1. Put some paper towels in the bottom of each plastic cup.

2. Pour 15 mL (3 tsp) of water into the bottom of each cup so that the paper towel is damp. Number the cups from 1 to 4.

3. In each cup, push a bean to the bottom of the paper towel. Cover it with another layer of damp paper towel.

4. Place the cups on a windowsill. Water them each day for two weeks. Measure and record their growth.

	Day 1	Day 2	Day 3	Day 4	Day 5	Day 6	Day 7	Day 8	Day 9	Day 10
1										
2										
3										
4										

How Do Plants Grow? *(cont.)*

What To Do: *(cont.)*

5. What day did each plant grow roots, leaves, and stalks?

	Bean 1	Bean 2	Bean 3	Bean 4
Root appeared				
Leaves appeared				
Stalks appeared				

 **Next Question**

Use your school library or the Internet to research the life cycle of many different plants. Include shrubs, flowers, and trees.

 Notebook Reflection

Imagine you were the bean sprouts. Use words and drawings to describe what happened each day.

How Does My Grass Grow?

Name _____

What You Need: • two containers   • grass seeds

                       • soil   • other seeds

What To Do:

1. Think of some conditions that make life difficult for plants. Choose one condition and work out how to make a model of it.

_____

_____

_____

_____

_____

_____

2. Take some grass seeds and plant them in a container. Plant some other seeds in the other container.

3. Set up your containers in your difficult conditions.

4. Your teacher will set up containers in healthy conditions. These are called the control plants.

5. Watch the plants grow for two weeks. Choose a way to record what happens to the plants each day.

 **Next Question**

Make a chart to compare your plants, the control plants, and three other students' plants.

 Notebook Reflection

Write about the causes for the differences that you saw between your plants and the control plants.

How Can I Grow My Own Lunch?

Name _____

What You Need:
- seeds (alfalfa or cress)
- paper plate
- cotton
- water

What To Do:

1. Line the bottom of the plate with damp cotton.

2. Sprinkle the seeds over the cotton.

3. Cover any exposed seeds with more damp cotton.

4. Leave the plates in a light, warm, and airy place and keep the cotton damp (but not wet). Watch the seeds grow for three weeks.

5. Draw what you see each week:

Week One

Week Two

What To Do: *(cont.)*

Week Three

Next
Question

These plants can grow on a paper plate and cotton. How might you grow other plants, like beans, onions, or tomatoes? How could you test your plan?

Notebook
Reflection

You could put these greens on a sandwich. What other parts of a sandwich can you make or grow yourself? How? Use words and drawings to explain.

How Are Seeds Different?

Name _____

What You Need: • seed sheet

What To Do:

1. Imagine you are an environmental scientist. Your job is to record the types of seeds in a national park. You can not collect samples. You must record descriptions of seeds.

2. The school grounds will be your national park. Search the school for different kinds of seeds.

3. Fill in the table for each kind of seed you find.

drawing of seed	type of seed	place seed was found	number of seeds found

What To Do: *(cont.)*

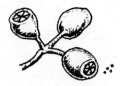

woody capsule

papery capsule

seed pod

berry

drupe

seed follicle

grain

nut

achene

cone

? Next Question

Use your school library or the Internet to research the kinds of seeds that you did not find. How are they similar and different than what you found?

📓 Notebook Reflection

Pick two or three kinds of seeds that you found. Describe each one in a short paragraph. Can you figure out how it "travels" to new places to grow?

How Do My Hands Work?

Name _____

What You Need: • colored pencils

What To Do:

1. List five things that you can do with your hands that you can't do with your feet.

_____

_____

_____

_____

_____

2. Lay your hand down on the desk next to this paper. Look carefully at your hand.

3. What do you think is inside your hand?

_____

_____

_____

4. How does your hand work?

_____

_____

_____

How Do My Hands Work? *(cont.)*

What To Do: *(cont.)*

5. Put your hand on the paper and draw around it. Then sketch what you think is inside your hand. Label each part you have drawn with its name and its use.

? Next Question

Research the interior of the hand. Find out how accurate your sketch was. What did you miss?

Notebook Reflection

Write a short paragraph describing how your feet are similar to and different from your hands.

How Many Bones Are in My Hand?

Name _____

What You Need: • colored pencils

What To Do:

1. Find a partner.

2. Look at the diagram of hand bones.

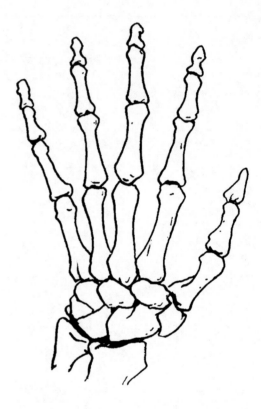

3. Feel your partner's hand. Try to feel the bones shown in the diagram. How many bones can you find?

_____

4. Use blue to color in the bones in the diagram that you found.

5. Use red to color in the bones in the diagram that you could not find.

 Next Question

Find a diagram of the bones in the foot. How many of those bones can you feel in your feet?

Notebook Reflection

Feel up your arm. Describe the bones you find. Find bones across your torso, legs, and neck.

How Can I Dissolve a Cookie?

Name _____

What You Need:
- crushed cookie
- lemon juice
- water
- two resealable plastic bags
- teaspoon

What To Do:

1. Place 5 mL (1 tsp) of crushed cookie into a plastic bag. Add enough water to just cover the cookie. This is your control.

2. Place 5 mL (1 tsp) of crushed cookie into the other bag. Add enough lemon juice to just cover the cookie.

3. Leave both bags overnight.

4. The next day, observe the crushed cookie in each bag. Tip some of the mixture out so that you can feel it with your fingertips. Describe what you see, feel, and smell.

water:

_____

_____

lemon juice:

_____

_____

 Next Question

Research the digestive system. How is the stomach similar to the experiment?

 Notebook Reflection

Why did the experiment call for two bags? Why was the control bag useful?

Ecology

This chapter provides activities that address McREL Science Standard 6.

Student understands relationships among organisms and their physical environment.

Knows the organization of simple food chains and food webs (e.g., green plants make their own food with sunlight, water, and air; some animals eat the plants; some animals eat the animals that eat the plants)	*Can We Balance an Ecosystem?* (page 101) *Can I Survive as a Consumer?* (page 104)
Knows that the transfer of energy (e.g., through the consumption of food) is essential to all living organisms	*Can I Survive as a Consumer?* (page 104)
Knows that an organism's patterns of behavior are related to the nature of that organism's environment (e.g., kinds and numbers of other organisms present, availability of food and resources, physical characteristics of the environment)	*How Do Mini-Beasts Work?* (page 106) *How Do Mini-Beasts Travel?* (page 108)
Knows that changes in the environment can have different effects on different organisms (e.g., some organisms move in, others move out; some organisms survive and reproduce, others die)	*Where Does Litter Come From?* (page 110)
Knows that all organisms (including humans) cause changes in their environments, and these changes can be beneficial or detrimental	*Where Does Litter Come From?* (page 110)

How to Teach Ecology

It's easy to forget that the natural world underpins our very lives, especially if you live in an urban environment. When your food comes prepackaged, and the only plants you see are in parks and flower shops, you can overlook the close relationship we all have with the natural world. Perhaps that's why we choose to take breaks in the countryside and succumb to the attraction of gardening. These activities bring us closer to the plants and animals we depend on.

Do Animals Need Plants?

We certainly do! Without plants, animals, including us humans, wouldn't survive—and I don't mean just because we eat them!

If we were dependent on the stored oxygen in the atmosphere for breathing, life on Earth would be finite. When the last of the oxygen had been used up (or actually, long before), most life on Earth would end. Even if we were to stop being so wasteful with the stuff—burning it or pumping it through our forms of transport—it would not last forever. It has to be renewed. Fortunately for us, green plants and algae are very good at that. All our oxygen is recycled again and again.

We would die long before the oxygen ran out, though. The reason for that is that the waste gas we breathe out—carbon dioxide—is poisonous in large quantities, and a buildup in the atmosphere would kill us. Fortunately, plants have a use for carbon dioxide. They recycle that too, using it to make food for themselves (and often, for animals) and produce oxygen!

This handy cycle ensures that life on Earth can continue indefinitely. True, plants need oxygen too, and yes, they produce some carbon dioxide, but this is far outweighed by the amount of oxygen they produce.

Plants give us more than just oxygen! We don't need plants just for gases. We can eat them (or we eat the animals that eat plants), and we use plant products for clothes, shelter, furniture, and medicines.

Without plants there would be no animal life on Earth. We need them. It is this complex relationship between plants and animals that makes their study so interesting.

It is the breakdown of this relationship, by pollution and the wholesale destruction of the rainforests, that threatens us and all other living things.

Do Plants Need Animals?

You wouldn't think so, would you? Everything they need is right there where they are growing. They have carbon dioxide from the air, water from the rain, and a pinch of mineral salts from the soil. Combining all these produces a living growing thing.

Do animals do anything for plants? Well yes, they do. They produce a large part of the carbon dioxide needed for plants to photosynthesize and live.

Just as important, animals provide a useful delivery system for living things that are literally rooted to the spot. If you have some dusty, yellow pollen that you are wanting to get to that plant over there, then what better way than hitching a lift on a furry insect traveling from flower to flower? Usefully, the honeybee has very casual standards of personal hygiene—and no clothes to brush. So it will fly off with pollen on its coat. Indeed, plants can even afford to sacrifice a bit as bee food—hence the pollen sacs on the bee's legs. Plants provide a few encouragements—sweet

How to Teach Ecology (cont.)

nectar, bright colors, and even markings (bee lines) that help with a safe landing.

Bees, flies, other insects, some birds, and other animals offer this helpful service—and it doesn't stop there. When the pollen has been delivered, the egg has been fertilized, and the seeds have formed, they need distributing, too. Animals also provide a convenient—if erratic—delivery service for seeds.

The outsides of animals—the fur of mammals and the feathers of birds—provide a convenient hanging place for hooked burrs and sticky seeds. The insides happily accept tasty fruits and, if the seeds are resistant to digestion (with a hard coat), they will pass through the eater and be deposited somewhere far away, together with some waste matter rich in organic material (otherwise known as manure).

Many seeds are transported like this. Even the huge stones of the avocado tree are carried away by the birds that eat the fruit—though it is probably just as well that they don't pass right through the bird but are regurgitated. Otherwise the resplendent quetzal bird might be famed for its constipation!

It's as if the fruits of many seeds had a sign hanging on them saying, "Eat me." Their color, taste, and smell are all inviting, and it doesn't take long before an animal accepts their invitation. And if they don't? The fruit falls to the ground with its precious packet of seeds and may germinate anyway. But, without the animals—especially the birds—that feast on their fruits and carelessly drop their seeds from the skies, a lot of plants would be rooted to the spot in every sense.

The Biosphere

Earth is packed with living things. Every plant and animal lives in an environment on Earth. One more name for this environment is the "biosphere." The biosphere is the part of our Earth that supports life—the land, the water, and the lower atmosphere.

A Habitat

A plant's habitat is its address—the place where it lives. An animal's habitat is its address, too. Because most animals move around, an animal's habitat is wider and bigger. A cave, a woodland, a pond, or a forest floor are all habitats. So are canals, gardens, and playgrounds.

Habitats are places that provide a source of raw materials for growth and activity; a source of energy, either from the sun or from the plants that harness the sun's energy; shelter from changing conditions, from weather and from predators; and a place to dump the products of living.

An Environment

We use the word "environment" to describe our surroundings on Earth. Our environment is everything that affects us—the place where we live, our home and school, our weather, our food, water, and the air we breathe, the plants and animals we affect and that affect us, the special animals we call our friends and family—and also the strangers whose work and behavior affect us.

The Ecosystem

The plants and animals in a habitat are linked through food chains and webs. The animals may live by eating plants found in their habitat or by eating other animals that in turn eat the plants. This link between plants and animals and their habitat is called an ecosystem.

Lions eat gazelles that eat the green plants found on the African plains. They are in the same ecosystem. Gazelles don't eat seaweed, and lions don't eat penguins. They are not found in their habitat and so are not a part of their ecosystem.

Energetic Ecosystems

Ecosystems are about energy flow. Forget any romantic view of nature. Think of the plants and animals as links in this flow of energy. The first link in this chain is the green plant kingdom. Plants capture the sun's energy through a process called photosynthesis, whereby they make their own food. This energy is passed on to animals who eat the plants (herbivores) and then to meat-eating animals that eat the herbivores (carnivores). At any stage, nutrients are returned to the soil through the decomposition of waste—excrement and dead bodies—and the cycle is complete. So even the soil and the physical surroundings are part of the pattern.

This is not an efficient process—each link in the chain needs to keep some energy for itself. The plants need to live and grow. So do the animals. In addition, creatures like us need to stay warm—an expensive business in terms of energy. We can waste a lot of this energy as heat loss, too.

The whole thing is pretty fragile. The removal of just one species can unravel the ecosystem with terrifying speed. That's why environmental protesters can get so hot under the collar. Take, for example, the spread of myxomatosis among rabbits. This disease was welcomed by farmers when it began to wipe out these cuddly pests. But the decimation of the rabbit population was catastrophic for foxes, who began

to look for food elsewhere, wandering suburban streets in search of full trash cans. At the other end of the scale, wild plant populations exploded, uncropped by rabbits. Suppose the fox population had been wiped out instead. The result would have been an explosion of rabbit numbers (remember, they would breed like rabbits!) and the green plants would be grazed to extinction. And then the starving rabbits would begin to die....

Food Chains

Why don't lions eat oranges?

Because they can't peel them, silly!

There are food chains in every habitat that ensure that organisms survive. You can see these food chains as a sort of energy flow and, ultimately, all that energy begins with the sun. It is the sun's energy that plants convert to their own structures, and hence to food. Green plants are the first link in most food chains.

After green plants, the next link is the plant-eaters. Finally, predators live off plant-eaters and also off each other. Food chains show how plants are eaten by plant-eaters, and plant-eaters are eaten by meat-eaters.

Of course, it's never quite as simple as that. Food chains with the direct line of the grass—zebra—lion type don't show the whole picture. Grass is eaten by more than just zebras; zebras eat more than just grass and are themselves eaten by more than just lions. And the lions eat more than just zebras.

Food Webs

It is easier to understand this in terms of food webs. Aphids live off plants and ladybirds live off aphids. But the ladybird could meet any number of

How to Teach Ecology (cont.)

fates from insect-eating birds, who might themselves take a fancy to a juicy aphid....

A food web shows the animals that might live on or around a tree for example. In every food web, there are many different food chains. The food web in a woodland, for example, might involve some plant-eating consumers like grasshoppers and mice. A secondary consumer like a frog might not tackle a mouse but will make a meal of a grasshopper. Snakes are partial to frogs, but not averse to a mouse or a grasshopper, either. Hawks will eat a snake—or jump that link and go straight for a mouse.

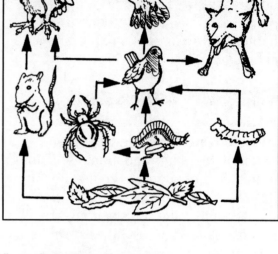

Just Another Bypass

Of course the biggest ecosystem destroyer has two legs—and giant earthmovers and an unlimited supply of concrete. When a new road is pushed through a habitat, it rattles not just the plants and animals living there, but others that depend upon them. Well-meaning conservationists have attempted to save habitats by moving them—rolling up a meadow to make room for a supermarket, for example. But other factors—the soil, the exposure, the microclimate—are different, and these projects are seldom successful. It's not just the plants and animals that matter. It's every aspect of the ecosystem. The more we learn about the environment, the more we discover how closely everything is interlinked.

Changing Habitats

Habitats change naturally. They may change daily, when the sun comes up and goes down, or the tide goes in and out. They may change with the seasons, as it turns first cold and then warm again. They may change completely over short

Fascinating Fact

Not all food chains start with a green plant. There are deep-sea life forms that can harness chemical energy. These bacteria live in total darkness near the hydrothermal vents of the Pacific Ocean, in very high temperatures. Deep-sea animals eat the bacteria as other animals eat plants.

periods of time: after an earthquake, a flood, or a volcanic eruption. They may change completely over a longer period of time, as a river changes course or rocks wear away. Ponds dry up, trees die and are replaced by new young trees, and grass withers in a hot summer.

Habitats are also changed by outside influences. Faced with yet another grazed knee, the principal of a primary school decided that the uneven paving slabs would have to go. A smooth layer of asphalt was the answer: no breaks, no gaps, no edges to trip over. The job was quickly done; but a small habitat was destroyed.

The small plants had had a grip on the thin soil between the slabs; ants had nested in the soft bedding sand; worms, beetles, and other small invertebrates lived under and between the stones. Birds were occasional visitors: the thrush that had found both snails and a handy anvil and the woodpecker that had feasted on ants when the tree insects were few. With the birds gone, the neighborhood cat no longer lurked with a view to catching a bird.

We can't help environmental change, but we can be sensitive to the rolling effects of our actions. On a much larger scale, desertification is the process that renders fertile land arid and dead. Around the world, a hundred square kilometers are lost to desert every day. In Africa, a series of droughts has enlarged the Sahara southwards. These droughts may be linked to world climate change. But heavy grazing and deeper wells have disturbed the fertile Sahel region, so that the Sahara is growing at around 5 km a year.

So, habitats are always changing. Most plants and animals can adapt to small changes in their habitat. But some cannot. Most animals can move when the habitat changes and find somewhere else to live. Plants cannot. Animals may survive seasonal change by migrating or by hibernating. Big changes to a habitat can destroy populations of animals and plants. Some of those big changes are made by people.

Extinction

Plants and animals that cannot adapt to changed conditions die out. And because humans have been responsible for more environmental change than any other factor, humans have been responsible for a great many extinctions. More animals have become extinct in the past 300 years than in all the years before because of humans. We have changed habitats by farming, clearing trees, and building roads and houses. Animals like the dodo, the Tasmanian wolf, and the Balinese tiger have died out.

We Can't Stop Change

Some of the most major changes are the result of the human factor. By our use of land, we can change habitats and affect the lives of plants and animals. Our changes may be damaging—green field site development—or for the better—the landscaping of old industrial sites. We are learning to protect environments, recognizing the delicacy of environmental balance and the vulnerability of the natural world.

This may go against your lifestyle. You may be an inner-city dweller who never sees a blade of grass. But you are as dependent on the environment as anybody. And remember—nowhere is without life. You just need to get out more and look around you!

How to Teach Ecology *(cont.)*

We are rightly concerned about environmental change—and especially environmental damage. But we would be wrong to think that habitats are unchanging. Every habitat is changing, even without human intervention. Animals and plants unable to survive these changes—annual, seasonal, or daily—will soon be extinct.

Can We Balance an Ecosystem?

Name _____

What You Need:
- food web cards
- colored pencils or markers
- calculator
- hole punch
- yarn
- scissors

What To Do:

1. Get in a group of four. Each student should take one blank card. Decide who will draw a producer, who will draw a primary consumer, who will draw a secondary consumer, and who will draw a tertiary consumer.

2. Draw a picture in the blank space and give it a name.

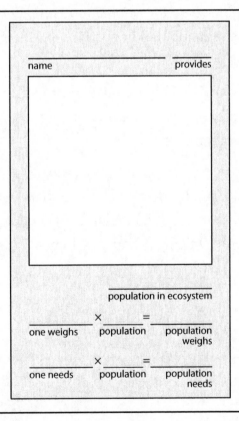

name _____   provides _____

_____
population in ecosystem

_____ × _____ = _____
one weighs   population   population
                                 weighs

_____ × _____ = _____
one needs   population   population
                                 needs

3. Decide how many of your organisms are in the ecosystem. Write that number in "population in ecosystem."

4. Estimate how much one organism weighs. Then multiply that number by the population to find the whole population's weight. Add these numbers to the card.

Can We Balance an Ecosystem? *(cont.)*

What To Do: *(cont.)*

5. Pick a number between 1 and 10 to represent how much energy your organism needs. Then multiply that number by the population to find out how much energy the whole population needs. Add these numbers to the card.

6. Divide the population's energy need by 10. This is how much energy the population provides other organisms that eat it. Add that number to the top of the card.

7. Now line up your group's cards with the producer on the bottom, then the primary consumer, then the secondary consumer, then the tertiary consumer. Punch holes in the tops and bottoms of the cards. Connect the cards with yarn.

8. Check each card to see if the population's energy needs are provided by the card below it. If that population needs more energy, punch a hole on the bottom of the card.

9. Check each card to see if the population provides more energy than its consumers require. If it provides more energy than is being consumed, punch a hole on the top of the card.

10. If you have any cards with open holes, repeat steps #2–#6 to make new organisms to fill those holes. Attach them to the web with yarn. Then do steps #8 and #9 to check that all the organisms get enough energy and that there isn't any extra energy being produced. Repeat until the web needs no more organisms.

❓ Next Question

Look at your completed food web. What would happen if one of those organisms was suddenly removed? What would happen if a new organism got dropped into the middle of the web?

📖 Notebook Reflection

Describe the steps you took to make a balanced web. Was it easy or hard? What made it easy or hard? How did you solve the problems you found?

Can We Balance an Ecosystem? *(cont.)*

Food Web Cards

name	provides

population in ecosystem

one weighs × population = population weighs

one needs × population = population needs

name	provides

population in ecosystem

one weighs × population = population weighs

one needs × population = population needs

name	provides

population in ecosystem

one weighs × population = population weighs

one needs × population = population needs

name	provides

population in ecosystem

one weighs × population = population weighs

one needs × population = population needs

name	provides

population in ecosystem

one weighs × population = population weighs

one needs × population = population needs

name	provides

population in ecosystem

one weighs × population = population weighs

one needs × population = population needs

Can I Survive as a Consumer?

Name _____

What You Need:
- 600 tokens
- green tags
- brown tags
- red tags

What To Do:

1. With the rest of the class, list ten primary consumers, ten secondary consumers, and ten tertiary consumers.

2. Divide the class into three groups. Two thirds of the class become primary consumers. One fourth of the class become secondary consumers. The rest become tertiary consumers.

3. Get a tag to show which group you are in. Primary consumers get green tags; secondary consumers get brown tags; tertiary consumers get red tags. You should also pick one animal from the list for your group. You will represent an animal of this species.

4. Spread the tokens in a large, open area. These represent food. In this lab, you will try to collect as many tokens as you can. Everyone must walk.

5. The primary consumers get a head start. They should collect as many food tokens as they can.

6. Thirty seconds later, the secondary consumers start. They can get tokens from the ground or they can "eat" other players by tapping their shoulder.

7. When an animal is eaten, both students sit down. The prey counts through their tokens. Every tenth token is given to the predator. The predator can stand up and collect more tokens; the prey must continue sitting.

8. Twenty seconds after the secondary consumers begin, the tertiary consumers may start. There will not be many food tokens on the ground; they will probably need to eat other animals for most of their food.

 **What To Do:** *(cont.)*

9. After two more minutes, the lab is done. Have each student count up how many food tokens they collected and say one thing about how they got their tokens or kept them safe.

 **Next Question**

What happens if some of the primary consumers only give predators one in twenty of its tokens? What happens if one of the secondary or tertiary consumers got more than one-tenth of the tokens from its prey? Rearrange the game and play again. What changes?

Notebook Reflection

Write a paragraph describing your experience in the game. What did you do? How did you get tokens, and how did you keep them? What were other students doing? Then write a paragraph describing how the game is similar to how animals act in a real ecosystem.

How Do Mini-Beasts Work?

Name _____

What You Need:
- mini-beasts
- tweezers
- trays
- sheet of clear plastic
- water
- sand
- flashlights
- rocks
- ruler

What To Do:

1. Put one mini-beast on the clear plastic sheet. Watch it from beneath. Write three words to describe how your mini-beast moves.

_____   _____   _____

2. Can the mini-beast move up a steep slope? Slope the tray and watch.

_____

3. How far can your mini-beast travel in thirty seconds? Mark where your mini-beast starts and time its movement.

_____

4. Does your mini-beast like light? Shine the flashlight at it. What happens?

_____

5. Use rocks, water, and sand to make a little world on the tray for your mini-beast. Watch your mini-beast travel through its world.

6. What does your mini-beast do when it meets water?

_____

7. What does your mini-beast do when it meets a big rock?

_____

How Do Mini-Beasts Work? *(cont.)*

What To Do: *(cont.)*

8. Draw the little world you made and mark your mini-beast's path through it.

Next Question

Design an even bigger and better landscape. Draw a diagram, and label the parts.

Notebook Reflection

Your mini-beast reacts to things like slope, light, water, and rocks. Why does it do what it does?

How Do Mini-Beasts Travel?

Name _____

What You Need: • mini-beasts

What To Do:

1. Go outside and find a mini-beast to follow.

2. Watch the way your mini-beast moves, eats, and rests. Draw and write your observations in the space below:

My mini-beast looks like this: _____

I found it here: _____

How Do Mini-Beasts Travel? *(cont.)*

What To Do: *(cont.)*

This is what it did first: _____

Then it did this: _____

3. Talk about your observations. Try moving like your mini-beast.

? Next Question

Use your school library or the Internet to research other ways that mini-beasts travel.

📔 Notebook Reflection

Write a story about where your mini-beast has come from and where it is going.

Where Does Litter Come From?

Name _____

What You Need:
- map of your school

What To Do:

1. Work with your class to make a list of different kinds of litter.

2. Work with a partner. Mark the areas on the map of your school where you think there will be litter.

3. Go outside. Pick up litter where you find it and mark it down. Use the chart on the bottom of this page.

Material	Description	Where was it?	Where does it come from?
paper			
plastic			
glass			
aluminum			
other			

What To Do: *(cont.)*

4. The area with the most litter was: _____

_____

5. The area with the least litter was: _____

_____

6. How correct were your predictions on where the litter was?

_____

_____

_____

7. Where does the litter come from?

_____

_____

_____

 **Next Question**

Make a plan to reduce the amount of litter in your school. Compare your plan with the rest of your class and come up with a master plan that every one can participate in.

 Notebook Reflection

On your way home from school, observe your surroundings. Where do you see litter? Where do you think it comes from? What can be done so there is less litter?

Diversity of Life

This chapter provides activities that address McREL Science Standard 7.

Student understands biological evolution and the diversity of life.

Knows that fossils can be compared to one another and to living organisms to observe their similarities and differences	*How Are Fossils Made?* (page 115) *What Is Amber?* (page 117) *What Can Tracks Tell Me?* (page 119)
Knows different ways in which living things can be grouped (e.g., plants/animals, bones/no bones, insects/spiders, live on land/live in water) and purposes of different groupings	*How Are Seeds Different?* (page 88)

How to Teach Diversity of Life

The Diversity of Life

There is a great deal of confusion as to how to organize all the living things on the planet. With ten million known species and millions more unknown species, that's hardly a surprise.

Morphological Classification

In the 1700s a Swedish scientist named Carl von Linné (or Carolus Linnaeus) invented a system to make sense of the way scientists group and name living things. The system is based on how similar and different living things are. He placed them in groups.

The groups contained organisms that look similar or have things in common. The largest groups are called kingdoms. Plants formed one kingdom; animals formed a separate kingdom. If it didn't move, it was a plant; if it moved, it was an animal. Linnaeus also had a third kingdom for minerals, which has since been discarded. New kingdoms have also been introduced—fungi were split off from plants, microorganisms from plant and animal kingdoms were regrouped into protoctista, bacteria, and archaea. Today there are six kingdoms.

The smallest groups are species—cows, tigers, and oak trees are all examples of species. Species are unique. Members of a species are a bit like the aristocracy; they breed with one another but (in normal circumstances) they can't breed with anyone else!

In between are phyla or divisions, classes, orders, families, and genera.

Linnaeus gave each species a two-part name. The two parts work like your surname and first name. They tell you which genus and species each living thing is. The ancient language of Latin is used for the names. This is so that everyone can understand them, no matter which language they normally speak. For example, the Latin name for a tiger is *Panthera tigris*. The genus is *Panthera* and the species is tigris. The scientific names are given group names first. Think of some student names and reverse them: Smith, Sharon, for example. Notice that the first, or generic, name always has a capital letter. The specific name always has a lower case initial letter. For example, *Homo sapiens*.

Cladism

However, morphological classification has some significant drawbacks. Since it is based on body structure, it groups organisms that look alike together. However, the fact that two organisms look similar is no guarantee that they actually live or behave in similar ways.

Cladism is an approach in which biologists group organisms based on their genetic ancestors. By studying DNA and evolutionary development, biologists are able to more precisely map how organisms came to be the way they are today.

The basic unit, the clade, is the group of organisms that share a single common ancestor. It includes all organisms that are descended from that ancestor.

Cladism and morphological classification overlap, and a great deal of developing science involves adapting morphological classifications to map to clades. For instance, all birds share a common ancestor, Archaeopteryx, and all descendants of Archaeopteryx are birds. Their class, Aves, is also a clade.

However, the reptile class Sauropsida is different. All of these organisms share a common ancestor—some proto-reptile of distant past—but not all of that proto-

How to Teach Diversity of Life *(cont.)*

reptile's descendants are in Sauropsida. There's a big group missing: the birds! Sauropsida is not a clade, but Sauropsida and Aves together are a clade.

Adaption

Only humans can adapt to almost any habitat. By wearing special clothes, living in special shelters or using technology, humans can live at the North Pole or in a desert, can go underwater, or can fly.

Each plant and each animal suits the place where it lives. You don't find monkeys under the sea or fish up trees. Monkeys and fish are adapted to their habitats.

An adaptation is a change in the way that plants or animals are shaped that suits them to their habitat. For example, while the eagle cannot reach the nectar inside flowers, it can soar high in the sky, has wonderful eyesight to help it spot its prey and fierce talons and a beak to catch it. The hummingbird cannot catch and eat other birds, but it is so tiny and has such an amazing speed of wing flapping that it can hover over flowers to feed on the nectar (and it can fly backwards—the only bird that can!).

Many animals fly but they fly in different ways. Hawkmoths can fly at 45 km an hour to escape predators. Swifts have small wings, adapted to flying at 170 km an hour to catch flying insects. Albatross don't fly so fast. Their huge wings—up to four meters across—are adapted to enable them to soar and glide for long periods.

All these different flying animals are adapted to living in different habitats. Each exploits its own environmental niche—usually very successfully, until some human comes along and messes it up.

How Are Fossils Made?

Name _____

What You Need:
- samples of fossils
- large bowl
- wooden spoon
- soil
- water
- natural objects (no plastic or metal)

What To Do:

1. What do you think fossils are?

_____

_____

_____

_____

2. Look at the fossil samples. How do you think they were formed?

_____

_____

_____

_____

3. Make an inland sea by placing soil in the bowl, adding water, and mixing it into mud.

4. Drop some natural objects into your inland sea.

5. Place the bowl in a sunny place for a few days to allow it to dry out.

How Are Fossils Made? *(cont.)*

What To Do: *(cont.)*

6. Break open your dried-out sea and examine the "fossils" you've made. Draw what you see.

7. Compare them with the fossil samples. What similarities and differences do you see?

_____

_____

_____

 **Next Question**

Use the library or the Internet to find out more about fossils. Where are they found? How old are they?

 Notebook Reflection

Imagine that you are dinosaur bones becoming fossils. Write what happens to you.

What Is Amber?

Name _____

What You Need:
- amber
- liquid gelatin
- clear plastic cup
- licorice strap or sheet
- water
- knives or scissors

What To Do:

1. Look at the amber. What is inside the amber? How could it have gotten there? What do you think amber is?

_____

_____

_____

_____

2. Half-fill your cup with liquid gelatin.

3. Describe what the gelatin looks like before it sets.

_____

_____

_____

4. Let the gelatin set.

5. Cut an insect shape out of the licorice. Set it on top of the set gelatin.

What Is Amber? *(cont.)*

What To Do: *(cont.)*

6. Pour more liquid gelatin into your cup to cover the insect shape. Let the gelatin set. Describe what you've made.

_____

_____

_____

_____

 **Next Question**

Research amber in the library or on the Internet. Find five interesting facts about amber.

 Notebook Reflection

Compare your gelatin model to the amber. Now what do you think amber is?

What Can Tracks Tell Me?

Name _____

What You Need:

- modeling clay
- large plastic bucket
- water
- spoon
- jug
- casting plaster
- cooking oil
- small paint brush
- newspaper
- bamboo stick
- sandpaper
- soapy water
- towel

What To Do:

1. Spread out the newspaper on your table.

2. Knead some clay until it is big enough for your foot to fit on. Brush the surface lightly with cooking oil.

3. Put your bare foot on the modeling clay and press down. Then clean your foot with the soapy water.

4. Now use some more clay to make a long, thin cylinder.

5. Wrap it firmly around the outside of the clay with your footprint to make a "wall."

6. Slowly pour the plaster into your footprint. Use the bamboo stick to push plaster into the narrow spaces of the footprint.

7. Tap the clay mold on the table to make sure there are no bubbles in the plaster.

8. Let the plaster dry for two hours.

9. Gently peel the clay away from the plaster. Smooth any rough edges of the footprint with sandpaper.

What Can Tracks Tell Me? *(cont.)*

What To Do: *(cont.)*

10. Compare your own foot to the footprint cast. What do you notice?

_____

_____

_____

_____

_____

_____

? Next Question

List all the things you can think of that you could tell about an animal that left a footprint.

Notebook Reflection

How do you think scientists use footprints to learn about the past?

Matter

This chapter provides activities that address McREL Science Standard 8.

Student understands the structure and properties of matter.

Knows that matter has different states (i.e., solid, liquid, gas) and that each state has distinct physical properties; some common materials such as water can be changed from one state to another by heating or cooling	*What Can Air Do?* (page 127) *How Strong Is Air?* (page 129) *How Fasts Do Cloths Dry?* (page 131) *How Does Fruit Float?* (see Teacher CD)
Knows that the mass of a material remains constant whether it is together, in parts, or in a different state	*What Are Different Soils Made Of?* (page 38)
Knows that substances can be classified by their physical and chemical properties (e.g., magnetism, conductivity, density, solubility, boiling and melting points)	*What Is a Conductor?* (page 132) *What is a Mixture?* (page 133) *How Acidic Is the Rain?* (page 135) *What Does Clean Really Mean?* (page 136) *What Is a Hydrometer?* (page 140) *How Can Dirty Water Get Washed?* (see Teacher CD)
Knows that materials may be composed of parts that are too small to be seen without magnification	*What Are Potato Chips Made Of?* (page 138)

How to Teach Matter

The world is full of stuff. In fact, it's made from stuff—including you, me, and this book. Scientists call this stuff matter—a confusing word if you are a student being told that something "doesn't matter." Because in the scientific sense, matter is the substance of the universe. It's all the stuff in the world: rocks, wood, plastic, and steel. It's rare and expensive, like gold and diamonds, or common and cheap, like soil and water. It's everywhere. Different materials have different properties.

By looking at the properties of materials, how they are used, and how they might be changed, this subject prepares students for their later understanding of chemistry.

It is important to tackle work on matter in a logical order. Only then can students understand that materials differ; that they can be grouped and classified in many ways; that this classification can help us to choose the right materials for a task; and finally, that there are ways of changing materials that make them suitable for a range of needs and tasks.

Particle Theory

Particle theory is simply the idea that everything is made up of very tiny bits, or particles. An understanding of this is enormously helpful when learning about materials. And it isn't difficult to understand.

A selection of great and good scientists were asked to imagine that all the science knowledge in the world was to be destroyed but they could save one piece of information. What would it be? Almost without exception, they chose the same idea—rejecting evolution, electricity, and Newton's laws of motion. The fact they wanted to pass on to succeeding generations was that all matter is made up of tiny particles.

Words like "atom," "molecule," and "particle" are in general use—sometimes correctly, sometimes not. Most young students could make a stab at explaining what particles are, or at least that they are "very, very small bits." Some might even know that they are mostly space. Understanding what particles are is a great help to understanding the behavior of materials.

Atoms

An atom is the smallest particle of a material that still retains the characteristics of that material. That is, a bar of iron is made of iron. Cut off a piece, and it's still iron. Cut off a piece of that piece, and it's still iron. You can keep cutting and cutting until you've got just one single iron atom—and it's still iron.

However, if you cut that atom in half, what you have ceases to be iron. What you would have is a collection of subatomic particles: protons, neutrons, and electrons. Now, if you really had split that iron atom, the subatomic particles would clump back together (after releasing a whole lot of fission energy) immediately. Those new groups of subatomic particles would be new atoms of different elements, no longer iron and no longer with the characteristics of that material.

Molecules

Molecules are groups of atoms which are chemically stuck together. The molecule often has different characteristics than the molecules that went into it. Sodium and chlorine, for instance, are quite poisonous—but sodium chloride, also known as table salt, is essential to human life.

How to Teach Matter *(cont.)*

Solid, Liquid, and Gas

Materials can be divided into solids, liquids, and gases. This isn't as easy as it sounds. There are some materials that behave in ways that put them in more than one group. Water, for example, can be found in all three states. In addition, it's very hard to prove to students that gases exist.

- If the particles are closely bonded together—able to vibrate but not part from each other—then the material is a solid.

- If the particles are close but not packed, so that they can move around, the material is a liquid.

- If the particles are widely spaced and move around, occasionally crashing into one another, the material is a gas.

These three are called the states of matter.

Liquid

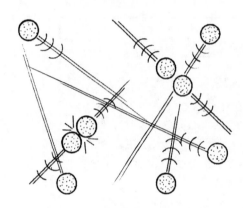

Gas

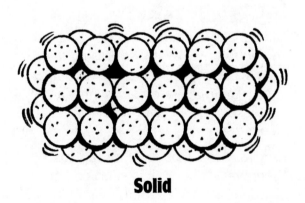

Solid

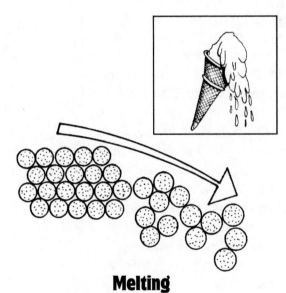

Melting

Changes with Temperature

The changes between the three states of matter are connected to changes in temperature. Increase the temperature, and a solid becomes a liquid, or a liquid a gas. Very occasionally, a solid becomes a gas without a liquid stage. Reduce the temperature, and gas becomes a liquid, or a liquid solidifies.

Fascinating Facts

And Glass Is a Liquid

Let's just get this one out of the way. It comes up later, but it's a favorite in trivia contests and among well-read students. Glass is a liquid.

Liquids flow. The thicker the liquid, the slower the flow. At room temperature, water flows freely while syrup flows slowly. Syrup has a higher viscosity than water. It takes an age to flow from the bottle. But glass has an even higher viscosity than syrup. You can't imagine windows made from syrup. But glass has such a high viscosity—it is so thick—that you can cut it into sheets and put it into windows. Over time, it flows downward. Clear evidence of thickening can be seen at the bottom of century-old windows. The bottom of the pane is thicker than the top.

Melting and Freezing

When solids melt, they become liquids. They can flow, pour, and fill a shape. Some solids melt when they are heated. Butter melts to become a liquid. Chocolate melts, too. Both become solid again when they are cooled. The cooling process is called freezing—even if it's not very cold to you or me.

Chocolate is not changed much by the melting, but butter loses water when it melts. The butter is changed by the melting. You can't change it back.

Evaporation and Condensation

Evaporation is the process by which a liquid turns into a gas. Extra heat jostles the liquid molecules around until they're so excited, they don't even stick together any more. They're now a gas.

Condensation is a process by which a vapor or a gas turns back to a liquid. Water vapor condenses on a cold window and collects in a liquid form again.

Changing Matter

The concept of materials changing is a difficult one. It's not surprising that students recognize changes when they are spectacular—a color change, a flame, smoke—but not when they are unexciting.

They may feel that "stuff disappears." There was a match, it was lit, and now it's gone. They may think that the product was somehow inside the original material—thus rust may be thought to ooze out of a corroding nail. They may simply think that one material has "turned into" another—the flour and water have turned into bread—without a word of explanation.

How to Teach Matter *(cont.)*

Sometimes we need to bring the material back to show that it was there all along.

Can You Make Bread from Toast?

Matter changes in two ways: physically and chemically. The difference between physical and chemical change is that whereas physical change is only a change in form—the substance is still there—chemical change is when new and irreversible substances are created. Sugar dissolving in tea is a physical change, but baking a cake is a chemical change.

Some physical changes are irreversible. Try sawing your leg off to see what I mean. No chemical change has taken place, but reattachment could be difficult.

So think of it this way:

Physical changes involve the rearrangement of particles: mixing, separating, putting them in a different state (solid, liquid, gas), or otherwise doing something to them without actually changing the particles themselves.

Chemical changes give you something new. The particles have been changed by splitting or combining with others or by changing partners so that they produce a new material you didn't have before.

So making sawdust is a physical change (which is irreversible), but making ammonia from hydrogen and nitrogen is a chemical change which is reversible—you can get the hydrogen and nitrogen back.

Although most physical changes are reversible and most chemical changes are not, there are exceptions!

Toast some bread. What kind of change happens? Can you reverse it? What is the material that forms on the surface of the bread? Burned toast is carbon. That's a new material, so the change is a chemical one. If you cut your toast in half, though, that change is physical—no new materials are made; the toast is just in two parts instead of one.

Does Salt Disappear in Water?

If you ask students what happens when something dissolves, they will often tell you that it "disappears." This seems to be true of materials that dissolve to make a colorless liquid—like salt or sugar. But dissolving instant coffee produces a material where the coffee has far from disappeared—it is clearly there throughout the changed, colored liquid.

Students' views may reflect their observations. Consider the following: "When I add sugar to my tea, it just disappears. You see the same thing when you add salt to water; first it's there and then it's not. The water won't weigh any more with the salt in it—it's just disappeared. You could go on adding salt if you liked. It would just go on filling the spaces."

Dissolving takes place when one substance is dispersed through another to become a single material. This material is called a solution. In theory, the substances involved could be solids, liquids, or gases. In practice, students will come across this most often when they add something solid to a liquid—for example, salt to water or sugar to tea. The solid and the liquid are called the solute and the solvent.

When a solid dissolves, it becomes dispersed throughout the liquid. If you were to sample any part of the liquid, you would find the solid there. This is not what happens when you add

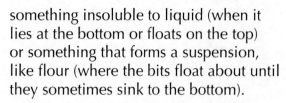

How to Teach Matter *(cont.)*

something insoluble to liquid (when it lies at the bottom or floats on the top) or something that forms a suspension, like flour (where the bits float about until they sometimes sink to the bottom).

When a white or colorless solid is added to water, it appears to disappear. Tasting safe materials in solution proves that the solid is still there. Colored solids may color the water, and the students can see how they color the whole of the solvent evenly.

Diffusion

Open a new air freshener, put it on a table, and then walk around the room. How quickly does the smell fill the room? Where do you have to stand so that you cannot smell it? Everything is made up of tiny particles. They are closely packed in solids, freer to move in liquids and freest of all in gases. How does that explain your air freshener?

The solid material in the freshener is losing particles. The particles are floating off and arriving in your nose, an organ designed to accept the tiny particles in a gas. Although your nose isn't in direct contact with the air freshener, you know it is in the room!

Can't Take Any More!

When the solvent cannot dissolve any more of the solute—the water cannot dissolve any more salt, for example— then the solution is saturated. Students may observe that salt will not go on dissolving in water forever. You can increase the amount of solute that the solvent will dissolve by raising the temperature of the solution, but as soon as the temperature falls, the solid comes out of solution again.

Raising the temperature of the solute and stirring are familiar ways of speeding up

dissolving. These two methods work because both encourage the release of the tiny particles of solid into the liquid. As a student once said when explaining dissolving, "If you dropped me in hot water and then hit me around the head with a spoon, I'd let go of my friends, too!"

Dissolving should not be confused with melting. Melting is the change of state from solid to liquid with increased temperature. Dissolving is one substance dispersing into another substance. However, some materials melt and dissolve simultaneously. Jelly can become a liquid and disperse through the water when stirred with hot water.

What Really Happens?

What happens to things that dissolve? Surely the salt has to go somewhere? When you add a solid that will dissolve to a liquid, it begins by filling the spaces between the particles of liquid. Rather like a theater with a fixed number of seats, the liquid will take so many arrivals before it is full. When it is full, the liquid can take no more, and is said to be saturated. The excess, like disappointed film-goers, is rejected and sinks to the bottom. Strangely, the level of the solute actually falls at first.

But some materials, like sand, don't dissolve. They may sink to the bottom of the liquid or, if they are low density, they may sit in mid-water or in suspension. If you put the liquid through a filter, only dissolved particles pass through. Large, undissolved particles are netted and stay behind. If you then let the water evaporate, you will be left with the dissolved solid, which may form crystals.

What Can Air Do?

Name _____

What You Need:
- plastic bags
- scales
- classroom objects

What To Do:

1. Fill a bag with air and tie it tightly. Put it on the floor.

2. Balance things from your classroom on the top. Try books, bags, and blocks.

3. Keep adding things until the bag of air can't hold them. How many objects did you get up to?

   _____

4. Find the weight of the objects that made the bag of air go flat. How much did they all weigh together?

   _____

Draw your bag of air and the things you put on top of it.

What Can Air Do? *(cont.)*

What To Do: *(cont.)*

5. Try sitting on the bag of air! What happens?

_____

_____

_____

_____

_____

Next Question

What happens when you use two bags of air? Can two bags of air hold up twice as much weight or more? What about three? Four?

Notebook Reflection

What can you now say about air? What does it do? How does it act? What can it be used for? Use words and drawings in your reflection.

How Strong Is Air?

Name _____

What You Need:
- clear plastic jar
- paper
- bowl of water
- towel

What To Do:

1. Scrunch up the paper very tightly.

2. Squash it into the bottom of the jar so when you turn the jar upside down, the paper does not fall out.

3. Turn the jar upside down. Keeping it straight, lower it into the bowl of water. Does the paper get wet?

_____

4. Draw what you have done in three steps, explaining what the water, the paper, and the air inside the jar were doing.

Step One

_____

_____

_____

_____

_____

How Strong Is Air? *(cont.)*

What To Do: *(cont.)*

Step Two

_____

_____

_____

_____

_____

Step Three

_____

_____

_____

_____

_____

 Next Question

Use your school library or the Internet to research a diving bell. How is it similar and different?

Notebook Reflection

Brainstorm different ways you can take what you learned in the experiment and use it in the real world.

How Fast Do Cloths Dry?

Name _____

What You Need:
- three identical pieces of cloth
- water
- string
- pegs

What To Do:

1. Dip the three pieces of cloth in water. Then squeeze out as much water as you can.

2. Choose places to hang the cloths. Put one somewhere you think it will dry quickly and one somewhere you think it will dry slowly. Keep one towel separate as a control.

3. Check the cloths every ten minutes. Record how long it takes each cloth to dry.

We put the first cloth _____ to dry quickly.

It took _____ to dry.

We put the second cloth _____ to dry slowly.

It took _____ to dry.

We put the last cloth _____ as a control.

It took _____ to dry.

 **Next Question**

Think of ways to dry the cloths more quickly and more slowly. Try out your ideas.

 Notebook Reflection

Why do you think cloths dry slower or faster?

What Is a Conductor?

Name _____

What You Need:
- C battery
- electrical wire
- light bulb
- block of wood or styrofoam
- two steel nails
- hammer
- paper clip
- small objects

What To Do:

1. Hammer the two nails into the block, 2 cm (1 in.) apart.

2. Use electrical wire to attach the battery to one nail. Attach the light bulb to the other nail. Then use a third piece of wire to connect the light bulb to the other end of the battery.

3. Place a paper clip across the nails on the block. The light should turn on. The paper clip is a conductor.

4. Now test to see if any of the small objects are also conductors. Place each one across the nails on the block. Record your results.

item	conductor?

 Next Question

What happens when you use more than one object to connect the nails?

 Notebook Reflection

Look over your results. Can you make any generalizations about what is a conductor and what isn't?

What Is a Mixture?

Name _____

What You Need:
- warm water
- 4 plastic cups
- sugar
- sand
- salt
- dirt or potting soil
- teaspoons
- strainer

What To Do:

1. Place a few grains of salt in the first cup, sand in the second cup, sugar in the third cup, and dirt in the fourth cup.

2. Fill one cup with warm water halfway. Stir the mixture. Describe what happens to each grain.

   Salt Cup: _____

   _____

   _____

3. Repeat for the other three cups. What happens?

   Sand Cup: _____

   _____

   _____

   Sugar Cup: _____

   _____

   _____

   Dirt Cup: _____

   _____

   _____

What Is a Mixture? (cont.)

What To Do: (cont.)

4. Use the strainer to pour the liquid out of each cup. What is left over in the cups?

Salt Cup:

_____

Sand Cup:

_____

Sugar Cup:

_____

Dirt Cup:

_____

 **Next Question**

What happens when you put more than one thing in a cup of warm water? What happens when you strain the results?

 Notebook Reflection

Use words and pictures to describe your results. Why do you think that the different materials got different results?

How Acidic Is the Rain?

Name _____

What You Need:
- bucket
- ruler
- 3 plastic jars
- tap water
- rain
- vinegar
- litmus paper

What To Do:

1. Attach the ruler to the inside of a bucket to make a rain gauge.

2. Place the rain gauge outside in an open area. Record the rainfall each day.

3. Fill one jar with tap water, one with rain water, and the other with vinegar. Label each jar.

4. Place a piece of litmus paper in each jar. Observe and record what happens to the litmus paper.

The litmus paper in tap water _____

_____ .

The litmus paper in rain water _____

_____ .

The litmus paper in vinegar _____

_____ .

The most acidic liquid was _____ .

Next Question

What is the acidity of other liquids in your daily life? Test water you find in swimming pools or in the ocean. Test juice, milk, and chicken soup! What else could you test?

Notebook Reflection

Vinegar is an ingredient in lots of the things you eat. Is it safe to eat an acid? Why or why not?

What Does Clean Really Mean?

Name _____

What You Need:

- four plastic containers with lids
- four identical cloth samples
- dirt
- three different detergent samples
- warm water
- teaspoon

What To Do:

1. Label four containers: Test 1, Test 2, Test 3, and Test 4.

2. Rub a pinch of dirt into three of the cloth samples. Make sure each cloth is equally dirty.

3. Put one sample in each container. Half fill the containers with warm water.

4. Add 5 mL (1 tsp) of detergent sample to each container. Use a different detergent in each. The last container should get no detergent.

5. Record which detergent went in which container.

Test 1: _____

Test 2: _____

Test 3: _____

Test 4: _____

What To Do: *(cont.)*

6. Shake each container as you count to 50. Remove and rinse the cloth samples. Make sure to keep track of which cloth was in which container. Describe the cloths:

   Test 1: _____

   Test 2: _____

   Test 3: _____

   Test 4: _____

7. Which detergent did the best cleaning the cloth?

   _____

 ## Next Question

Why did one container have no detergent? Research experimental control. Find three other examples.

 ## Notebook Reflection

Which detergent would you buy? What reason might make you buy a different detergent from the experiment?

What Are Potato Chips Made Of?

Name _____

What You Need:
- four different samples of potato chips
- spoon
- squares of brown paper

What To Do:

1. You will create and perform an experiment to test the oil content of different chips. There are four variables to use: chips, brown paper, time, and oil content. There is only one variable that you want to change. The others you want to stay the same so they do not affect your results. Write how you will keep three variables the same and allow one to change:

   Chips: _____

   Brown Paper: _____

   Time: _____

   Oil Content: _____

2. Write a plan for your experiment.

   _____

   _____

   _____

   _____

   _____

 #50164— *Standards-Based Investigations: Science Labs—3-5*

What Are Potato Chips Made Of? *(cont.)*

What To Do: *(cont.)*

3. Make a hypothesis. Which chip do you think will have the most oil? Which will have the least?

_____

4. Perform your experiment. Describe what happens.

_____

_____

_____

_____

_____

 **Next Question**

How could you make your experiment better? Try the experiment again with four new kinds of chips.

 Notebook Reflection

Describe the questions and answers that you had to ask yourself in creating your experiment.

What Is a Hydrometer?

Name _____

What You Need:
- straw
- nail
- waterproof glue
- tall glass jar
- water
- salt
- milk
- cooking oil
- waterproof pen

What To Do:

1. Squeeze the glue into one end of the straw and then slide the nail through the glue. If necessary, seal the nail in with more glue. Let the glue dry. This is your hydrometer.

2. Fill the jar with water. Slide your hydrometer into the jar, nail first. Use the pen to mark the straw at the water surface.

3. Remove your hydrometer and label the mark "Water."

4. Repeat steps #2 and #3 with saltwater, milk, and cooking oil instead of water.

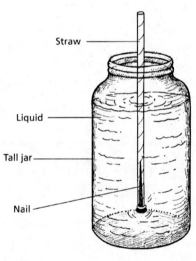

Straw

Liquid

Tall jar

Nail

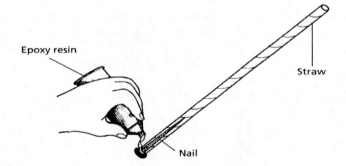

Epoxy resin

Straw

Nail

 Next Question

Repeat the experiment using ice water and very hot water. What changes?

 **Notebook Reflection**

Why do you think your hydrometer floated at different levels?

Energy

This chapter provides activities that address McREL Science Standard 9.

Student understands the sources and properties of energy.

Knows that heat is often produced as a byproduct when one form of energy is converted to another form (e.g., when machines and living organisms convert stored energy to motion)	*How Powerful Is the Sun?* (page 150)
Knows that heat can move from one object to another by conduction and that some materials conduct heat better than others	*How Powerful Is the Sun?* (page 150) *How Does Heat Travel?* (see Teacher CD)
Knows the organization of a simple electrical circuit (e.g., battery or generator, wire, a complete loop through which the electrical current can pass)	*How Does a Flashlight Switch Work?* (page 147) *What Does Positive and Negative Mean?* (page 149)
Knows that light can be reflected, refracted, or absorbed	*How Many Reflections Are There?* (page 152) *What Is Fiber Optics?* (page 154) *How Does the Magic Candle Work?* (page 155) *What Can Sun Damage Do?* (see Teacher CD) *How Do Colors Combine?* (see Teacher CD)
Knows that the pitch of a sound depends on the frequency of the vibration producing it	*How Does Sound Work?* (page 157) *What Is a Rommelpot?* (page 159) *What Are Sound Waves?* (see Teacher CD) *How Does a Voice Box Work?* (see Teacher CD) *How Is Music Made?* (see Teacher CD)

How to Teach Energy

Students will have a great deal of experience with energy but a difficult time identifying what energy they encounter every day. Many will suggest electricity, but they also encounter heat, light, and sound every minute of every day of their lives.

Heat and Temperature

Temperature is a measure of how hot something is, not how much heat there is in it. A bucket of hot water may have considerable heat in it, but it is not at the same high temperature as a light bulb or a sparkler firework.

Thermometers measure the level of heat in degrees. There have been several scales for measuring temperature, but the most common is the Celsius scale, named after Anders Celsius. This scale calls the freezing point of water 0° C, and the boiling point of water 100° C.

If the sun is shining through the windows, or the heat is on, you may be warm. If the windows and doors are open, and the heat is off, you may be feeling chilly. If you have a thick sweater on, you may be warm, even if the room is cold. Several factors determine how cold you may feel—how cold the room is, how warm your body is, and how warm the heater is. To know each of these factors, we have to compare temperatures with the temperature of our bodies. However, our bodies are not accurate measuring instruments.

You can see this for yourself by conducting the following short experiment. Fill three bowls with water. Fill one from the hot tap (not too hot!), one from the cold tap, and one using half hot and half cold water. Put your bowls in a row: hot, warm, and cold. Put one hand in the hot water and one in the cold. Count to ten. Now put both hands in the warm water.

What do you notice? Because one hand has become used to hot water and the other to cold, they don't do a very good job of telling you how warm the warm water is. Why is using your body a poor way of measuring temperature? While a thermometer will give you an objective measure, based on a defined scale, your hands relate the temperature to previous experiences. The hand that has been in cold water senses the warm water as hot. The hand that has been in hotter water senses the warm water as cold. We have all had this sort of experience in the swimming pool, moving from toddler pool to main pool, from pool to hot shower. The sea can also feel very cold after you have been sitting on a warm beach.

Light

Light is a form of energy. The energy of light is called radiant energy. To radiate means to send out rays or waves. Only a certain type of radiant energy can be seen with the human eye. We call this visible light.

We can see because of light. Light bounces off objects and travels to our eyes. Our eyes and brain work together to translate that light into what we see.

How Light Is Made

Everything is made of very tiny particles: atoms and molecules. Heat causes particles to become excited and move faster. The excited particles then radiate light.

Have you ever seen the bottom of a pan that is heating on the stove? Did it look like the hot pan was turning colors? When heated, the atoms on the surface of the pan start to bump into each other. This causes them to give off extra energy. This radiant energy is what scientists call light.

Light travels in waves much like water moves in waves. The amount of energy that a wave carries determines the color of the light. Waves differ from each other in length, rate, and size. These are called wavelength, frequency, and amplitude. Wavelength relates to the color of the light.

What happens when a light wave hits the atoms that make up everything? Several things might happen.

- The light can change direction, or refract.
- Some of the light rays can reflect off of the surface.
- The light can be absorbed into the material.

Refraction

Light rays bend as they travel through the surface of transparent material. Transparent means that light can be seen through it and move through it. This bend in the light is called refraction. It occurs when light travels through different materials at different speeds.

Reflection

The return of a wave of energy after it strikes a surface is called reflection. Smooth and polished surfaces like mirrors reflect more light than surfaces that are rough or bumpy.

When light reflects from a smooth surface, all of the light rays reflect in the same direction. A mirror is smooth, so you can see your image in it. When light reflects from a rough surface, the rays reflect in many directions. It is

impossible to see your reflection in paper, because the surface is rough.

Absorption

When it comes to color, absorption is the key. Look at the clothes you're wearing. What colors are they? The truth is, the colors are not in the clothing. The colors come from reflected and absorbed light. We see the colors because of the light that is reflected and sent to our eyes.

You know that light is made of waves. Each color has its own frequency. When visible light strikes an object, each frequency behaves differently. Some frequencies are absorbed. They are not seen. Some are reflected. The reflections are what appear as the color or colors of an object.

White light is made of all the colors of the rainbow. These colors are red, orange, yellow, green, blue, indigo, and violet. Some people know the colors as ROYGBIV. Now, look at something red. You can see just by looking at it that the object absorbs the frequencies for OYGBIV. But R, or red, is reflected. Your eyes pick up that reflection, and you see the object as red.

The important idea is that the color is not in the object. It is in the reflected light.

Sound

Sound comes from vibrations. Just like with light, atoms within substances move. Their movement creates sound waves. As the waves move through matter, they cause vibrations. The vibrations are picked up by the ear and sent as impulses to the brain. The brain translates them as the sounds we hear.

Sound Waves

Not all sound waves are alike. The

differences let us hear various sounds. Scientists have discovered that sounds and sound waves differ in the following ways:

- Wavelength is the distance between the troughs on either side of a single wave.

- Amplitude is measured in the height of the sound wave. It relates to the loudness or softness of a sound. When a wave is high, the sound is loud, and the amplitude is large. When a wave is low, the amplitude is small and the sound is soft.

- Frequency of sound relates to speed. The number of cycles per second that waves pass a given location is the frequency. The brain understands frequency as pitch. Fast vibrations cause high pitch. Slower vibrations make lower-pitched sounds. A tweeting bird makes a high-pitched sound. A roaring lion makes a low-pitched sound.

The Speed of Sound

Sound waves pass through all forms of matter. These include gas, liquid, and solid. The speed of sound changes as the waves pass these different states of matter. Sound waves move:

- slowly through gases.

- more quickly through liquids.

- fastest through solids.

Temperature also affects the speed of moving sound waves. Higher temperatures cause sound to move faster. At normal room temperatures, sound travels about 343 meters per second. That is like traveling 1,217 kilometers per hour!

The Doppler Effect

As you've read, pitch is the highness or lowness of sound. The frequency of a sound determines its pitch. High-pitched sound has a higher frequency. Low-pitched sound has a lower frequency.

Have you ever noticed that the pitch of a fire truck's siren is high when it comes toward you? Then it is lower as it passes and moves away. What causes this?

As the fire truck approaches you, the waves reach you more frequently. The pitch is higher than if the fire truck were not moving.

This pitch change, which was caused by a moving object, is called the Doppler effect. The firefighters on the truck do not hear any change in pitch. Their distance from the source of the sound does not change. The Doppler effect only comes into play when the distance changes.

Electricity

How Does the Battery Work?

It's a common misconception that batteries are somehow full of electricity. Some students think that connecting them up in a circuit uses all this electricity up, and then the battery is empty or "dead." But that's not how it is.

Electricity is a flow of minute particles called electrons, passed hand to hand like "pass the parcel." These electrons are in the materials that make up the circuit, but the battery provides the "push" that makes the electrons flow.

The energy for the push of a battery comes from chemical reactions in the battery. It's when these chemicals have all changed and there is no longer the material for the chemical reaction that we say the battery is dead.

Understanding the Flow of Electricity

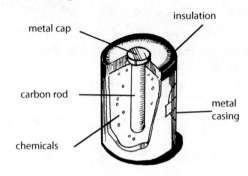

metal cap

insulation

carbon rod

metal casing

chemicals

The mistaken idea that electricity rushes out of the battery or the wall outlet, dashes to the radio, does its job, and disappears exhausted is not helped by the fact that a single cable operates most electrical appliances. Electricity apparently flows into the device to be "used up." You might show the students a piece of unconnected two-strand wire to show that electricity flows to a device and back again. There are two wires inside the cable.

The way electricity flows is affected by the components in the circuit. The electric current in a circuit is exactly the same wherever you decide to measure it. If there was electricity staggering back to the battery, you might expect there to be weak or strong points. But electricity flows a bit like water from a pump. The battery is the pump pushing the electricity around.

Complete Circuits

A circuit must be complete for the electricity to flow. All the components, linked in a complete circuit, are needed for a bulb in the circuit to light. Look closely at a flashlight bulb (when the light is off!). The wire filament inside is part of the circuit. The electricity flows right through the bulb.

Electric current has a direction from the negative to the positive terminal of the battery. When it was first investigated, it was thought that it flowed from positive to negative. However, this has now been shown not to be the case. And it certainly doesn't flow in both directions at once (the idea of "clashing currents" that students sometimes hold) despite the battery having two terminals.

An Analogy of an Electrical Circuit

You may need to use an analogy to explain the flow of electricity in a circuit to students. There is evidence that analogies help students to understand the invisible flow of electricity, but no analogy is perfect.

Use a loop of rope to represent the circuit. A student pushing the rope around in a circle represents the battery. If another student in the ring holds the rope more tightly, they create a resistance. They are behaving like a light bulb. An analogy of a switch would be a very tight grip on the rope: a resistance that no amount of pushing will overcome.

The bulb lights because the moving electrons collide with the fixed atoms in the thin filament wire (the filament wire resists the flow of the electrons). The moving electrons transfer energy from the battery to the bulb. The bulb glows—because it is in a glass globe that contains no oxygen, it can't burn away.

The wiring inside the bulb completes a full circuit. The more electricity flowing through the bulb, the brighter the bulb is. Students may think that a large battery will make a bulb brighter. Higher voltage batteries do tend to be larger, but size alone is not an indicator of voltage—for example, 1.5V batteries exist in several different sizes.

How to Teach Energy *(cont.)*

Caution!

It is essential to explain the safe use of wall outlet electricity devices early. Many students will have routine home experience of their use. Do not encourage exploration or investigation of wall outlet electricity. Explain that wall outlet electricity is dangerous and can be lethal.

How Does a Flashlight Switch Work?

Name _____

What You Need:
- C battery
- electrical wire
- lightbulb
- paper clips
- piece of cork or styrofoam

What To Do:

1. Use the battery, wire, and lightbulb to make the bulb light up. Draw your design.

2. Disconnect one wire from the battery. What happens?

_____

_____

How Does a Flashlight Switch Work? *(cont.)*

What To Do: *(cont.)*

3. Now use the paper clips and cork to make a switch. The switch should turn the lightbulb on and off. Draw your design.

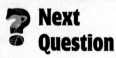 **Next Question**

Compare your switch with other students' switches. What are the similarities? What are the differences?

 Notebook Reflection

Did your first idea for step #1 work? How about step #3? How did knowing what didn't work help?

What Does Positive and Negative Mean?

Name _____

What You Need:
- two C batteries
- electrical wire
- electrical tape
- LED (Light Emitting Diode)

What To Do:

1. Look at your batteries. Find the end marked with a **+**. Find the end marked with a **–**.

2. Tape the two C batteries side-by-side so that one **+** end is next to a **–** end. Connect one **+** end to another **–** end with electrical wire.

3. Look at your LED. You will find one of two things. Some LEDs have two leads of different lengths. The long lead is the **+** lead. The short end is the **–** lead. Other LEDs will have thick and thin leads of the same length. The thin lead is the **+** lead. The thick lead is the **–** lead.

4. Use electrical tape to connect the **+** and **–** ends of the battery to the **+** and **–** leads of the LED. Does it matter which end of the battery is connected to which lead of the LED? Why?

_____

_____

_____

 **Next Question**

Make a cardboard model of a creature. Use one or more LEDs to make the model light up.

 Notebook Reflection

Why do you think batteries and electrical devices have + and – parts?

How Powerful Is the Sun?

Name _____

What You Need:
- four samples of sunscreens
- ultraviolet light
- fluorescent markers
- scissors
- paper

What To Do:

1. Cut the paper into four quarters. Use a fluorescent marker to draw four colored stripes on each piece.

2. Turn on the ultraviolet light. Put one piece of paper under the light. What happens to the colors?

_____

_____

_____

_____

3. Remove the paper. Carefully color the stripes on the paper with one sunscreen sample. Label which sunscreen you use on the paper.

4. Put the paper back under the ultraviolet light. Record your observations.

_____

_____

_____

_____

What To Do: *(cont.)*

5. Repeat the experiment with the other sunscreens on the other pieces of paper. Record your observations.

_____

_____

_____

_____

 **Next Question**

Research the effects of sunburns. How do sunscreens work?

 Notebook Reflection

Which sunscreen do you think is the best? Why?

How Many Reflections Are There?

Name _____

What You Need:
- two flat mirrors
- clear tape
- protractor
- candle
- matches
- modeling clay

What To Do:

1. Use tape to hinge the two mirrors together.

2. Use a protractor to set the mirrors at a 90° angle.

3. Place a lit candle in front of the two mirrors. How many images do you see?

_____

_____

4. Reduce the angle to 60°, then 45°, then 30°. What do you see each time?

60° _____

_____

45° _____

_____

30° _____

_____

5. Is there a relationship between the angle and the number of images?

_____

What To Do: *(cont.)*

6. Separate the two mirrors and place them parallel and facing each other. Use modeling clay to hold them in place.

7. Place the candle between the two mirrors and look into one mirror from slightly above or slightly to one side. How many images do you see?

_____

 ### Next Question

Can you find the mathematical relationship between the angle of the mirrors and the number of candles you see?

 ### Notebook Reflection

Draw a diagram of the mirrors and candle. Draw a line showing how light from the candle reflects on the mirrors to your eyes.

What Is Fiber Optics?

Name _____

What You Need:
- clear tape
- scissors
- black construction paper
- fiber optic light guide
- flashlight

What To Do:

1. Cut out a circle of black paper to fit over the reflector end of the flashlight. Cut a small hole in the center and tape the paper in place on the flashlight.

2. Turn the flashlight on and place the end of the light guide over the hole. What do you observe at the other end of the guide?

_____

_____

_____

3. Why do you think you see this?

_____

_____

_____

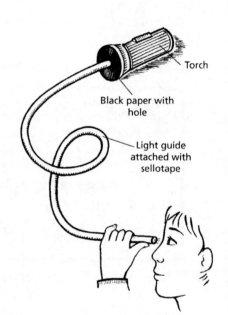

Torch

Black paper with hole

Light guide attached with sellotape

 Next Question

Research Morse code. Slide the light guide under a door, and have your friend sit on the other side watching the light. Can you send a message to your friend?

Notebook Reflection

Draw what you think happens inside the light guide. How is the light guide different from a cardboard tube? What might be going on inside? How could you test your idea?

How Can I Make a Magic Candle?

Name _____

What You Need:
- pane of glass
- modeling clay
- two candles
- index cards
- ruler
- two pins
- glass of water
- sheet of paper
- match or lighter

What To Do:

1. Use modeling clay to hold up the pane of glass across the middle of the sheet of paper.

2. Use the ruler to mark off every 2 cm (1 in.) away from the glass.

3. Place a pin in each candle to act as a marker. Drip some candle wax on each index card and place the candle on top of it. When the wax cools, the index card and the candle should move as one object.

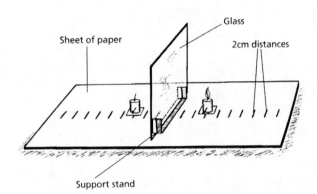

4. Place each candle on either side of the paper so that they are the same distance from the glass.

5. Sit down at one end of the paper. Light the candle closest to you. What do you notice about the other candle? Can you explain why?

_____

_____

_____

_____

_____

What To Do: *(cont.)*

6. Move each candle back and forth along the line of marks. Draw what you see with the candles in three different positions:

Next Question

Reach around the glass to touch the unlit candle. What do you see? Describe how this could be used in movies.

Notebook Reflection

Based on the experiment, what can you conclude about the reflection of light?

How Does Sound Work?

Name _____

What You Need:
- rubber bands
- several different tuning forks
- table

What To Do:

1. What do you think sound is? How could you test or prove what you think?

   _____

   _____

   _____

2. Stretch a rubber band between your thumb and forefinger. Pluck it. Describe what happens.

   _____

   _____

   _____

3. Stretch the rubber band as tightly as you can. Pluck it. Describe what happens now.

   _____

   _____

   _____

4. What is different when the rubber band is stretched out?

   _____

   _____

   _____

How Does Sound Work? *(cont.)*

What To Do: *(cont.)*

5. Tap the open end of the tuning fork against the edge of the table. Then hold it standing up with the end on the table. What do you observe?

_____

_____

_____

6. Repeat step #5 with different tuning forks. What do you find out about the sounds each one makes?

_____

_____

_____

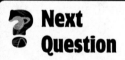 **Next Question**

Stretch a number of rubber bands out to different lengths. Pluck them. What do you find?

 Notebook Reflection

Now what do you think sound is? How does the experiment support your idea?

What Is a Rommelpot?

Name _____

What You Need:
- string
- match
- plastic sheet
- can
- water

What To Do:

1. Tie the end of a piece of thin string around the middle of a match.

2. Make a small hole in the center of the plastic sheet and thread the free end of the string through the hole.

3. Pour a little water into the can. Spread the plastic sheet over the top end and tie it down with string. Pull the ends down under the string to make sure it is tight.

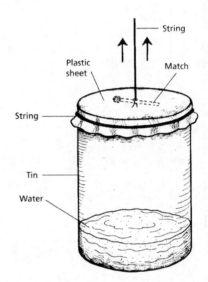

4. Hold the can in one hand. Take the string in your other hand, between your thumbnail and fingernail. Draw your hand upwards. Describe what happens. What do you think causes this?

_____

_____

_____

 Next Question

Open your rommelpot and pour more water into it. Seal it up and pull on the string again. Do you get a different result?

Notebook Reflection

Describe what is happening. Where do the vibrations come from? How do we perceive those vibrations?

Forces and Motion

This chapter provides activities that address McREL Science Standard 10.

Student understands forces and motion.

Knows that magnets attract and repel each other and attract certain kinds of other materials (e.g., iron, steel)	*What Is Magnetic?* (page 166) *What Holds Up the Magnet?* (page 168) *Where Does the Magnet Point?* (page 170) *How Can Magnets Be Used?* (page 171) *What Is a Magnetic Field?* (page 173) *How Can I Escape Friction?* (page 175) *Which Way Does the Tube Point?* (page 176) *How Do Electromagnets Interact?* (page 177)
Knows that the Earth's gravity pulls any object toward it without touching it	*What Falls Fastest?* (page 179) *What Makes Balancing Easier?* (see Teacher CD) *How Does a Tumblebug Work?* (see Teacher CD) *How Tall Can I Build It?* (see Teacher CD)
Knows that electrically charged material pulls on all other materials and can attract or repel other charged materials	*What Does Electricity Do to Magnets?* (page 180) *What Is an Electromagnet?* (page 181)
Knows that an object's motion can be described by tracing and measuring its position over time	*What is a Single Fixed Pulley?* (page 183) *What Is a Single Moving Pulley?* (page 184) *What Is a Block and Tackle?* (page 185) *Where Are They Now?* (see Teacher CD)
Knows that when a force is applied to an object, the object either speeds up, slows down, or goes in a different direction	*How Much Can I Change?* (page 186)
Knows the relationship between the strength of a force and its effect on an object (e.g., the greater the force, the greater the change in motion; the more massive the object, the smaller the effect of a given force)	*How Are These Two Eggs Different?* (page 188) *What Is a Wheel?* (page 189) *How Far Does It Roll?* (page 190)

How to Teach Forces and Motion

So What Are Forces?

Forces are behind everything that is happening around us. Forces make things happen.

You probably think this subject is difficult. You are quite right to fear getting too deeply into it because when you do, you will have to suspend your disbelief and your trust in common sense. Forces just don't behave as we would expect them to. Teaching forces is not easy!

Take these examples. Which of them would you think are true?

1. Two balls the same size dropped together from the top of the Leaning Tower of Pisa will both hit the ground at the same moment, even if one is a foam ball and the other is made from lead.

2. A bullet fired horizontally across a field from a gun, and an identical bullet dropped at the same moment from the barrel, will both hit the ground simultaneously.

3. When you sit on a table, it pushes back at you with an equal and opposite force.

4. There are two forces acting on a kicked football once it is in the air—the drag of the air and the downward pull of gravity.

5. The force of gravity is pulling you downward, but you are also pulling Earth towards you with your own force of gravity.

That's right—all of them are true.

Well, almost.

Position, Velocity, and Acceleration

One of the more obscure foundations of physics is position and its derivatives velocity and acceleration. It is very easy to overlook the simple proposition that things have positions, and those positions change. However, all of forces and motion requires this foundational understanding in order to actually work.

Position

Position is where an object is. That position cannot be measured absolutely—that is, there is no position that describes where the object "really is." Instead, position can only be measured relative to other objects. The blue block is three inches from the red block. The text stops a half-inch from the edge of the page.

Velocity

Velocity is the rate at which position changes. Students will probably be familiar with the idea of speed. Velocity is speed plus a direction: not 50 kph (31 mph), but 50 kph (31 mph) due east.

Acceleration

Acceleration is the rate at which velocity changes. Students may be familiar with the word accelerate, thinking that it means "speed up." However, acceleration is any change in velocity: speeding up, slowing down, or changing direction.

Pushes and Pulls

Forces are pushes and pulls. You can't escape forces—they are around you all the time.

When you are cycling, you need to push on the pedals to move forward. The ground is pulling on your tires to slow you down. The air is pushing in your face. If you stop pedalling, the ground and the air will slow you down until you come to a stop, but their forces keep working.

Attach a trailer on the back of the bike. Now you are pulling. Your force on the trailer is a pulling force. You push the pedals; the bike pulls the trailer! Stop cycling and try sitting still. Surely no forces are acting now? In fact, the force of gravity is pulling down on you. And the ground is pushing back.

The ground? Pushing? Yes, it has to. If the ground didn't push back, you would fall to the middle of Earth. So the ground pushes on your bike, and your bike pushes on you. Good thing, too. You don't want to disappear into Earth!

Faster and Slower

You use forces when you change speed. Hop on a scooter. First, you want to accelerate. Push off with your foot. The ground is pushing back at you and you're away! Want to go faster? It's no good just thinking about it. A bit of force is needed. Foot down, push again, and again. That's better. Now you are really rolling.

Lamppost ahead. Time to slow down. Push your foot to the ground. Slowing… whoops! Bit of a mistake there. The lamppost is still coming up. Brakes on. Put foot down and push backwards. Too late. Contact. Unfortunately, the lamppost pushed back just as hard as you pushed on it. It certainly stopped you.

Changing Direction

You can't change direction without a force, either. It might be the push and pull you give to the scooter handlebars. It might be the push and pull you give to a steering wheel. It might be the twisting

force you give to your leg as you jump sideways to catch a ball. (You can see the results of that force if you look at the soles of your shoes. Old shoes get a well-worn jumping-off spot.)

Isaac Newton, the great scientist, stated this as a law in 1687. He said that every object would remain still, or carry on moving in the same direction at a steady speed, unless forces acted on it. This is called Newton's first law of motion.

It doesn't matter whether it is speeding up, slowing down, or changing direction, you need forces for change! Forces make things change direction. Try bouncing a ball. It changes direction when it hits the ground or the wall. But the new direction can be predicted. Try rolling a ball against the wall and seeing which way it bounces off. What do you notice? You can predict the angle— especially if you are a good billiards player!

Two Special Forces

There are two special forces. They are also invisible. They don't need to touch an object. They can act on an object without touching it. They are magnetism and gravity.

Magnetism

Magnets exert forces. The forces act on magnetic materials. Some metals, like iron and steel, are magnetic but not all metals are magnetic. Magnetic metals can be attracted over a distance. Magnets can repel other magnets, too. They can push other magnets over a distance.

Gravity

Gravity works over a distance, as well. All objects have gravity. But for those of us on Earth, the gravitational pull of Earth is the nearest and strongest by far.

Earth's gravity holds us on the planet. If you drop something, it will always fall downward. Earth's gravity pulls it down.

Is Magnetism Magic?

Magnets are magical and mysterious—a sure winner with students. They are also excellent subjects for investigations. All you need are a few well-chosen questions.

How Is a Magnet Made?

A material like iron is made up of countless tiny bits, all of them magnets. Usually, these little bits are facing randomly, like people crowded into a room. When the iron is made magnetic, all the magnetic bits face the same way. It's as if you open a window at one end of the room, and everyone turns to face it.

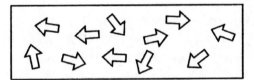

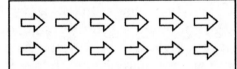

But heat a magnet, give it a good bashing, or let little Jimmy drop it on the classroom floor a few times, and all the magnetic bits will end up facing randomly again. Your magnet is weakened or destroyed. It's a good idea to put your magnets away with "keepers." These bridge the ends or poles of a pair of magnets and ensure that the magnetic force is circled and enclosed. Your magnets will last a lot longer if you do this!

Earth Is a Magnet

Four hundred years ago, a scientist named William Gilbert made a dramatic suggestion. He had looked at the way magnets turned to face north-south. This would happen, he argued, if Earth itself were a huge magnet.

He was right. Around every magnet there is an area, a field, where the invisible force of magnetism is operating. Earth has its own magnetic field. It has poles, just like any other magnet, which are not quite in the same places as the true north and south of Earth.

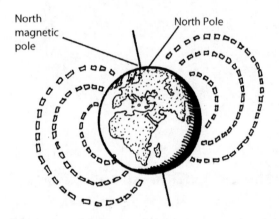

Electromagnets

The connection between electricity and magnetism was discovered in a classroom. In 1820, Hans Christian Oersted was teaching about electricity when he brought a magnetic compass close to the wire. To his amazement, the compass needle moved suddenly to line up with the wire. He realized that the electricity through the wire was making its own magnetic field.

There is a magnetic field around any wire that carries an electric current. Electromagnets have this wire coiled around a metal core. Electromagnets are magnets that can be switched on and off. When they are off, they are just iron bars inside a coil of insulated wire. When they are switched on, they become powerful magnets that can lift scrap metal, ring doorbells, and pull a steel splinter from your eye.

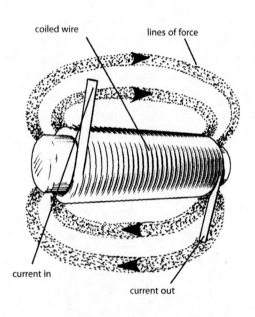

Can a Magnet Make Electricity?

Electricity plus magnetism produces movement. And movement plus magnetism will produce electricity. If electricity flows through a wire, it produces magnetism and can move a magnet. And the reverse is true. If you move a magnet near a wire, then you generate electricity. You are doing just this if you have a dynamo-powered light on your bike. As you cycle along, you are providing the movement, and the moving magnets in the dynamo generate electricity for the bulb.

This was Michael Faraday's shattering discovery. Without this form of electricity generation, only batteries would provide our electricity. His invention changed the world. Electricity generators contain magnets. When you

make the magnets move using a steam turbine, moving water, or the power of the wind, you generate electricity.

Gravity and the Apple Tree

We all dream that we could be as clever as the great scientist Sir Isaac Newton." If only an apple fell on my head," we think, "it would rattle my brain. I could have some brilliant ideas like him."

Bad news. The apple never fell on Newton's head.

Thousands of artists have drawn the apple conking poor old Isaac, and a light bulb lighting up. Idea! Now I can explain gravity.

Sadly, it wasn't like that. As Newton explained to a friend, he was walking in an orchard, puzzling over the problem of gravity, when an apple fell." Why does that apple fall downwards?" he thought. "Why does everything fall downward? It's as if there is a force pulling everything towards the center of Earth."

And there is. That force is gravity. It pulls everything towards the center of Earth. Everything has a force of gravity. The bigger it is, the bigger the force. But the biggest, nearest thing to you is Earth. Without gravity, nothing would stay on planet Earth that wasn't nailed down.

Earth's gravity is pulling down on us all the time. We call that pull your weight. You have weight because Earth's gravity is pulling down on your mass. The mass is the stuff you are made from. Your mass stays the same, wherever you are. But your weight can change.

If you went to another planet, the pull of gravity would change. If that planet were bigger than Earth, the pull would be stronger. If it were smaller than Earth, the pull would be weaker.

How to Teach Forces and Motion *(cont.)*

Can Heavy Things Fall Slowly?

Everyone finds it very hard to believe that light and heavy things, dropped together, can hit the ground together. Even when you've seen it, you may not believe it! Earth pulls harder on things of greater mass, and you might expect them to fall faster. But their greater mass means they're harder to get moving (just compare pushing a bicycle with push starting a car) and these two just about cancel each other out. Whatever the mass, objects fall at the same speed.

The exception, of course, is where one object has a greater surface area than another, catching the wind. A sheet of paper will float to the ground more slowly than a wadded-up ball; a feather will fall much more slowly than a hammer. The Moon astronauts graphically demonstrated what happens without the slowing effects of the air. A feather on the airless Moon dropped at the same speed as a hammer.

Balanced Forces

You can't see the forces acting on a football. They're invisible. One is the force of gravity. Gravity is pulling the ball down towards the center of Earth. So why doesn't the ball go down? Something is stopping it. The ground is pushing back on the ball. Gravity and the push of the ground are in balance. The ball stays where it is! When two forces are in balance, an object stays still. A space rocket on the launch pad has two forces acting on it—that of gravity pulling it down, and that of the launch pad pushing it up. These forces are in balance, and the rocket stays still. Until the engines start….

Floating and Sinking

Some objects float in liquids. Some sink. Some objects can be made to float, or they can be made to sink.

Objects float when they are lighter than the liquid. Even heavy objects can be made to float, as long as they are filled with air. The air makes them lighter than the liquid. When things are lighter than the liquid, the upthrust of the liquid holds them up. Gravity pulls down. The liquid pushes up. The two forces are in balance. The object stays still. It floats.

A floating object is in balance. The force of gravity is balanced by the upthrust of the liquid. As long as the object isn't too dense—when the force of gravity will exceed the upthrust of the liquid and the object will sink—the object will float, the forces on it nicely balanced.

When Are Forces Unbalanced?

When forces are unbalanced, things move. Take that space rocket. It is blasting off at John F. Kennedy Space Center. It is being held back by gravity, but gravity is a weak force compared to the tremendous thrust of the rocket engines. Because the forces are unbalanced, the rocket climbs into the sky.

When forces are unbalanced, things change shape. When you squeeze some modeling clay, the modeling clay pushes back. But if the modeling clay pushed back as hard as you squeezed, you could never change its shape.

What Is Magnetic?

Name _____

What You Need:
- bar magnets
- small objects

What To Do:

1. Use your magnet to find objects that are attracted to it. List or draw them in the boxes below:

things attracted to the magnet	things not attracted to the magnet

What To Do: *(cont.)*

2. Look at the magents and objects on the table. Suggest a way to move one magnet without touching it.

_____

_____

_____

3. Try your idea. Describe how well it works.

_____

_____

_____

 **Next Question**

Hold one magnet up to another. What happens? Now reverse the magnet. What happens now?

 Notebook Reflection

What did the things attracted to the magnet have in common? Form a hypothesis of what is attracted to magnets.

What Holds Up the Magnet?

Name _____

What You Need: • two bar magnets

What To Do:

1. Lay one magnet on the table. Hold the second magnet so its north pole is above the first magnet's north pole.

2. Slowly lower the second magnet until one end is on the table and the other end floats above the first magnet. Describe the process.

_____

_____

_____

_____

_____

3. What happens if the top magnet is not in exactly the right place?

_____

_____

_____

_____

_____

What Holds Up the Magnet? *(cont.)*

What To Do: *(cont.)*

4. What happens if you turn the floating magnet around?

_____

_____

_____

_____

5. What holds up the floating magnet?

_____

_____

_____

_____

_____

 **Next Question**

Compile a list of things that use magnets.

 **Notebook Reflection**

Write the rules of a game that uses magnets.

Where Does the Magnet Point?

Name _____

What You Need:
- bar magnet
- metal rod
- styrofoam
- tape
- plate
- water
- compass
- thread
- stand

What To Do:

1. Stroke one end of the magnet along the metal rod, from top to bottom. Repeat 20 times, always in the same direction.

2. Tape the rod to a small piece of styrofoam.

3. Float the styrofoam in a plate of water. Note which direction the rod points.

The rod points at _____ .

4. Gently spin the styrofoam in the water. Wait until the rod stops moving. Where is the rod pointing? Do this three times.

First, the rod pointed at _____ .

Then, the rod pointed at _____ .

Lastly, the rod pointed at _____ .

5. Hang the bar magnet from the stand using the thread. Where does the magnet point?

_____

6. Examine the compass. Where does it point?

_____

_____

 Next Question

Research the Earth's magnetic field. Explain how what you find is related to the experiment you did.

Notebook Reflection

Describe what you think is happening. Why do you think the ends of magnets are named north and south?

How Can Magnets Be Used?

Name _____

What You Need:
- magnetic toys
- two bar magnets
- construction materials (glue, cardstock, markers, string, tape, etc.)

What To Do:

1. Examine the toys. Look at how they work. Hold the magnets up to the toys. Does this change how they work?

_____

2. Design your own magnet trick, toy, or game. Draw and label your design below:

 **What To Do:** (cont.)

3. Explain how your design works. Use the words "attract" and "repel."

_____

_____

_____

4. List the materials you will need to make your design.

_____

_____

_____

5. Make your design.

 Next Question

Show your design to other students. Ask for ways to improve it.

 **Notebook Reflection**

Write a short paragraph describing how you use magnets every day.

What Is a Magnetic Field?

Name _____

What You Need:
- two bar magnets
- iron filings
- sheet of clear plastic

What To Do:

1. Place the plastic sheet over a bar magnet. Sprinkle the iron filings on top of the sheet. Draw what happens.

S   N

What Is a Magnetic Field? *(cont.)*

What To Do: *(cont.)*

2. Remove the sheet. Scatter the iron filings around on the sheet.

3. Place another magnet next to the first as in the diagram below. Put the sheet back on top. Describe what happens.

| S | | N | | N | | S |

_____

_____

_____

4. Remove the sheet and scatter the iron filings again.

5. Turn one magnet around so they look like the diagram below. Put the sheet back on top. Describe what happens.

| S | | N | | S | | N |

_____

_____

_____

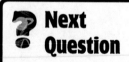
Next Question

What happens when you add a third magnet? A fourth? What shapes can you make with magnets and filings?

Notebook Reflection

What do you think is moving the iron filings around in patterns? Where does it come from?

How Can I Escape Friction?

Name _____

What You Need:
- electric motor
- battery
- cork
- drill
- thread
- glue
- paper clip
- magnet
- some books or spacers

What To Do:

1. Drill a hole through the center of the cork so that it fits snugly on the shaft of the motor. Push the shaft into the larger end of the cork about half way through.

2. Push one end of the thread into the other end of the hole. Add a drop of glue to keep it in place.

3. Tie a paper clip to the other end of the thread. Let the glue dry.

4. Connect the motor to a battery and place them on top of a book. Place the magnet on top of the book some distance away from the motor. The paper clip should almost reach the magnet.

5. Move the magnet back and forth until the paper clip is suspended in the air beside it. Turn on the motor. Draw what happens.

 Next Question

Using classroom resources and the Internet, research friction and machines. Why would a frictionless bearing be useful? Why is friction something that you might want to escape?

Notebook Reflection

Imagine a machine that uses a frictionless bearing like the one that you just made. Draw it and describe what it would do. Be sure to highlight how the frictionless bearing is used.

Which Way Does the Tube Point?

Name _____

What You Need:
- copper wire
- battery
- cardboard tube
- tape
- plastic dish
- bin of water

What To Do:

1. Wind about 20 turns of copper wire into a coil around the cardboard tube. Peel the plastic coating off of the ends of the wire.

2. Place the coil in the plastic dish beside the battery. Attach the bare ends of the wires to the battery with tape.

3. Float the plastic dish in the bin of water. What direction does the coil point?___

4. Turn the dish to point another way. What happens? _____

_____

 **Next Question**

Float two dishes in the same bin of water. What happens? Why?

 Notebook Reflection

Compare the experiment with a hiking compass.

How Do Electromagnets Interact?

Name _____

What You Need:
- copper wire
- cotton spools
- knitting needle
- battery
- electrical tape
- switch
- compass

What To Do:

1. Coil 30 turns of copper wire around each cotton spool, leaving a few inches free on either end.

2. Put each spool on the knitting needle. Twist the two inside ends of wire together.

3. Connect the other ends of the wires to the battery and switch, as shown in the diagram.

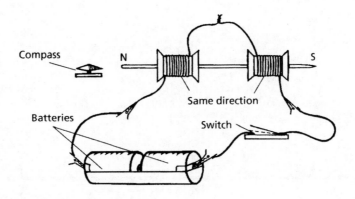

4. What happens when the switch completes the circuit?

_____

_____

_____

What To Do: *(cont.)*

5. Hold a compass near each end of the knitting needle. Which end of the compass points towards each end?

_____

_____

_____

6. Take one of the spools off the knitting needle, turn it around, and put it back on the needle. Repeat steps #4 and #5. What has changed?

_____

_____

_____

 **Next Question**

Stack three electromagnets together on the knitting needle, or bring two knitting needles with electromagnets together. How do they all interact now?

 Notebook Reflection

Describe in pictures and words how the electromagnets interacted. Can you draw any conclusions about how they work together?

What Falls Fastest?

Name _____

What You Need:
- sheets of paper
- balls large and small
- boxes large and small

What To Do:

1. Carefully stand on a chair. Drop a flat sheet of paper. Describe how it fell.

_____

2. Scrunch another sheet of paper into a ball. Drop it. Describe how it fell.

_____

3. Which of these objects do you think will fall the fastest?

flat paper	scrunched paper	small ball	large ball	small box	large box

4. Design a test to find out. How can you find the answer?

_____

_____

_____

5. Which one fell the fastest?_____

Which one fell the slowest?_____

 **Next Question**

How can you make the boxes fall faster or slower?

 Notebook Reflection

Why do you think you got the results you did? Use words and drawings to describe how it all works.

What Does Electricity Do to Magnets?

Name _____

What You Need:
- 9-volt battery
- C batteries
- compass
- copper wire
- switch

What To Do:

1. Use copper wires to connect the C battery to the compass, the compass to the switch, and then the switch back to the other end of the battery.

2. Observe what happens to the compass needle when the switch connects the wires. Describe what you see.

_____

_____

3. Replace the C battery with the 9-volt battery. Each end of the wire should connect to a different plug on the top. Switch the circuit on again. Describe what you see. Is there any difference?

_____

_____

 **Next Question**

Collect a number of different sized batteries. Read their outside wrappers. How many volts (labeled with a "V") does each provide? Does the size of the battery determine how many volts it provides?

 Notebook Reflection

Why does one battery have a different effect than the other battery? Imagine a third battery. What results would you get with that battery? What is different about the battery that produces different results?

What Is an Electromagnet?

Name _____

What You Need:
- C battery
- 9-volt battery
- copper wire
- paper clips
- plastic straw
- plastic-coated electrical wire
- aluminum foil
- long steel screw

What To Do:

1. Wrap the copper wire around the screw just once. Connect the ends to the C battery. You have made an electromagnet.

2. Touch the screw to a pile of paper clips. How many paper clips does the electromagnet pick up? _____

3. Repeat steps #1 and #2 with different numbers of turns around the screw. Record your results.

number of turns	number of clips for a C battery	number of clips for a 9-volt battery

What To Do: *(cont.)*

4. Repeat the experiment using the 9-volt battery.

5. What conclusion can you make regarding the strength of the electromagnet, the number of coils, and the voltage of the battery?

_____

_____

6. Replace the copper wire around the electromagnet with aluminum foil. Then wrap the plastic-coated wire around the foil-wrapped screw. How does this affect the electromagnet?

_____

_____

7. Replace the screw with the plastic straw. How does this affect the electromagnet?

_____

_____

8. What combination of materials makes the strongest electromagnet?

_____

9. What combination of materials makes the weakest electromagnet?

_____

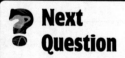 **Next Question**

Straighten one paper clip. Slide it into the plastic straw. Wrap the copper wire around the straw and connect it to the battery. What happens? Why?

 Notebook Reflection

Describe in words how each part of the electromagnet affects its strength: the battery, the wire, the number of coils, the screw or straw, and the foil wrapper.

What Is a Single Fixed Pulley?

Name _____

What You Need:
- pulley
- 15 cm (6 in.) wire
- 40 cm (15 in.) string
- sinker or weight
- meter stick
- support stick
- screw eye

What To Do:

1. Screw a screw eye into the middle of a support stick.

2. Make a U shape with the wire. Thread the pulley onto the wire, and then twist the ends of the U closed. Leave 5 cm (2 in.) free above the twist.

3. Bend the extra 5 cm (2 in.) into a hook. Hang the wire and pulley from the screw eye.

4. Tie one end of the string to the sinker. Thread the other end through the pulley.

5. Pull down on the string to raise the weight. Describe what happens. How far do you have to pull? How hard do you have to pull?

_____

_____

_____

6. Tie an identical sinker to the free end of the string. Try lifting one weight, then the other. Can you balance the weights? What does this tell you about the pulley?

_____

_____

 Next Question

Try the experiment again with different weights. What changes?

 Notebook Reflection

Describe a situation where a single fixed pulley would be useful.

What Is a Single Moving Pulley?

Name _____

What You Need:
- pulley
- 15 cm (6 in.) wire
- 40 cm (15 in.) string
- sinker or weight
- meter stick
- support stick
- screw eye

What To Do:

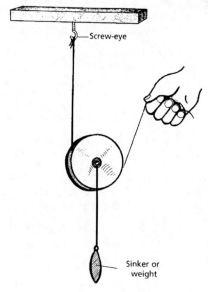

Screw-eye

Sinker or weight

1. Screw a screw eye into the middle of a support stick.

2. Make a U shape with the wire. Thread the pulley onto the wire, and then twist the ends of the U closed. Leave 5 cm (2 in.) free above the twist.

3. Bend the extra 5 cm (2 in.) into a hook. Hang the sinker from the hook.

4. Tie one end of the string to the screw eye. Thread the other end through the pulley.

5. Pull up on the string to raise the weight. Describe what happens. How far do you have to pull? How hard do you have to pull?

_____

_____

_____

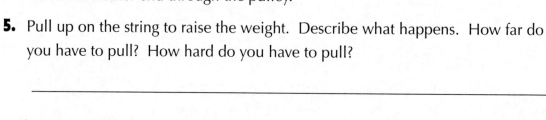

Next Question

Try the experiment again with different weights. What changes?

Notebook Reflection

Describe a situation where a single moving pulley would be useful.

What Is a Block and Tackle?

Name _____

What You Need:

- four pulleys
- sinker or weight
- meter stick
- support stick
- screw eye
- 40 cm (15 in.) string
- two lengths of 15 cm (6 in.) wire

What To Do:

1. Screw a screw eye into the middle of a support stick.

2. Make a U shape with one wire. Thread two pulleys onto the wire, and then twist the ends of the U closed. Leave 5 cm (2 in.) free above the twist.

3. Bend the extra 5 cm (2 in.) into a hook. Hang the wire and pulley from the screw eye.

4. Make another U shape with the other wire. Thread two pulleys onto the wire, and then twist the ends of the U closed. Leave 5 cm (2 in.) free above the twist.

5. Bend the extra 5 cm (2 in.) into a hook. Hang the sinker from the hook.

6. Thread the string through the set of pulleys as shown in the diagram.

7. Pull down on the string to raise the weight. Describe what happens. How far do you have to pull? How hard do you have to pull?

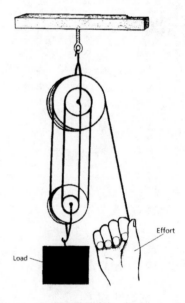

Effort

Load

_____

_____

 Next Question

Try the experiment again with different sized pulleys. What changes?

Notebook Reflection

Compare and contrast using a single pulley and using a block and tackle.

How Much Can I Change?

Name _____

What You Need: • modeling clay

What To Do:

1. Shape the clay into a sausage shape.

2. Push the ends of the sausage inwards. Draw what happens.

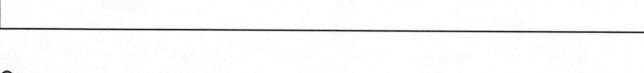

3. Make the sausage again, then slowly pull it apart. Draw what happens.

How Much Can I Change? *(cont.)*

What To Do: *(cont.)*

4. Make another sausage. Give it a twist. Draw what happens.

5. What changes do you make to the clay? What doesn't change about the clay?

Changes

_____

_____

Doesn't Change

_____

_____

? Next Question

What other materials besides clay could you do this experiment with? Would you get different results? Try it!

Notebook Reflection

Can you push, pull, and twist your body? How do those movements feel? Do you change like the clay changes?

How Are These Two Eggs Different?

Name _____

What You Need:
- raw eggs
- hard-boiled eggs
- gentle ramp
- plates
- newspaper

What To Do:

1. Hold the raw egg at the top of the ramp and let go. Observe what happens and record it below.

2. Repeat the experiment with the cooked egg.

raw egg	cooked egg

3. Put a plate on a sheet of newspaper. Place a raw egg in the center of the plate. Make the egg spin.

4. Lightly place one finger on the spinning egg, then take your finger off. Record what happens below.

5. Repeat the experiment with the cooked egg.

raw egg	cooked egg

 **Next Question**

What other things can you do that make the eggs do different things?

 Notebook Reflection

Why do you think the two eggs act differently? Use words and drawings to explain.

What Is a Wheel?

Name _____

What You Need: • table   • rollers   • carpeted floor

What To Do:

1. Your teacher will turn a table upside down.

2. Have some students sit on the upside-down table. Have some other students push or pull the table across the carpet. How many pushers do you need for how many passengers?

Passengers	1	2	3	4	5	6
Pushers						

3. Watch your teacher place rollers under the table. Do you think it will be easier to push the table with or without rollers?

_____

4. Experiment with passengers and pushers again.

Passengers	1	2	3	4	5	6
Pushers						

5. Did you need fewer or more pushers with the rollers? _____

Were you right in step #3? _____

 Next Question

Use math to describe the relationship between passengers and pullers. What do you find?

 Notebook Reflection

Why do you think wheels changed the experiment? Use words and drawings to explain.

How Far Does It Roll?

Name _____

What You Need:
- ramp
- rollable things
- yardstick

What To Do:

1. Watch your teacher set up the ramp.

2. Roll different things down the ramp to see how far they go. Don't push them, just let them go.

3. Measure how far each thing rolls. Draw and write about the things you rolled.

object	distance

4. Which object rolled the shortest distance? _____

5. Which object rolled the longest distance? _____

 **Next Question**

How can you make things roll further? What changes can you make to the objects, to the ramp, or to the floor?

 Notebook Reflection

Look at your answers for steps #4 and #5. Why do you think those objects went those distances?

Investigate That Question!

Name _____

What You Need: • this worksheet

What To Do:

1. From a class lesson, copy one question that you think would be difficult to answer. Write why.

Question: _____

This is difficult because: _____

2. How could you design an experiment to find an answer?

Experiment:

_____

_____

_____

Prediction:

_____

_____

_____

 **Next Question**

Perform your experiment. Was your prediction accurate?

 Notebook Reflection

Are there any questions from your lesson which can't be tested?

References Cited

American Association for the Advancement of Science. 1989. Science for all Americans: A project 2061 report on literacy goals in science, mathematics, and technology.

American Association for the Advancement of Science. 1993. *Benchmarks for science literacy: Project 2061.* Oxford University Press.

Daniels, H., and S. Zemelman. 2004. Out with textbooks, in with learning. *Educational Leadership* (December 2003/January 2004):36–40.

Krueger, A., and J. Sutton. 2001. *EDThoughts: What we know about science teaching and learning.* Denver, CO: McREL.

Lemke, J. L. 1990. *Talking science: Language, learning, and values.* Westport, CT: Ablex.

National Academy of Science. National Science Education Standards. National Academy Press. http://www.nap.edu/readingroom/books/nses/.

Saul, E., ed. 2004. *Crossing borders in literacy and science instruction.* St Louis, MS: International Reading Association, Inc.

Their, M. 2002. *The new science literacy.* Portsmouth, NH: Heinemann.